Tammy has given the church a ~~~~~~~~~~~~~~~ courageous, convicting, and compassionate. *Choosing the Opposite* is not just an invitation to rethink our assumptions; it's a road map back to the radical heart of Jesus' Kingdom. Reading this book felt like sitting across from a trusted friend who loves Jesus deeply and wants to help you live like him too. With pastoral wisdom and prophetic clarity, Tammy helps us confront our cultural entanglements and rediscover a way of living that is beautifully upside down. Rooted in the Sermon on the Mount, this book will comfort the weary, challenge the comfortable, and guide us toward a faith that looks a lot more like Jesus. It's bold, honest, refreshingly clear—and exactly what the church needs right now.

IAN SIMKINS, lead pastor of The Bridge Church

Choosing the Opposite is a bold, countercultural master class that will make you laugh, cry, and crave the ways of Jesus. Tammy Melchien is a genius—her scriptural insights and prophetic voice have long inspired me. In this book, she brings the words of Jesus to life, offering a fresh, relevant, and deeply challenging path to follow. With wit, wisdom, and spiritual depth, she delivers an invitation to a richer, more meaningful way of living. You might as well buy multiple copies now because you're going to give this one away!

DANIELLE STRICKLAND, author, advocate, and speaker

The most important thing about this book is that Tammy Melchien lives out what she writes about. As a result, *Choosing the Opposite* is a book I highly recommend for everyone who is determined to live like Jesus in these challenging times. Make the choice!

GREG NETTLE, president of Stadia Church Planting

This book delivers a much-needed wake-up call for those serious about following Jesus in a world that often distorts his message. With sharp biblical insight, cultural awareness, and prophetic challenge, Tammy Melchien dares us to rethink our instincts, reject fear-driven faith, and embrace the radical way of the Kingdom. She challenges the status quo, exposing the ways we've been shaped by fear, power, and division rather than by Jesus himself. This book is a wake-up call for a compromised church and a road map for those who long to live differently. If you're ready to move beyond comfortable Christianity and follow Jesus with fresh conviction, read this book, wrestle with it, and seek to live it!

DEB AND ALAN HIRSCH, authors of missional discipleship, spirituality, and leadership resources and founders of Forge Mission Training Network and Movement Leaders Collective

When Jesus finished his now-famous Sermon on the Mount, the first response was one of amazement, and the second one was a kind of disagreement: The crowds recognized that Jesus exceeded their expectations for what Jesus could claim. Most of us, if we were but honest in our reading of the Sermon, would join the crowds in thinking that what Jesus says is counter to many of our expectations—which is the excellent angle taken in this book by Tammy Melchien, *Choosing the Opposite*. Here the reader will find a clear explanation of the Sermon on the Mount with one insight after another. What if we, in discovering the kingdoms that are shaping our lives, were to choose the opposite of the well-worn direction we have been traveling in this Christian-life journey? If we did, we just might find ourselves walking with Jesus. Over and over Jesus carved a path opposite of the ruling kingdoms of this world, and he calls us to choose his opposites. Excellent for small groups as well as for teachers and preachers preparing sermons.

SCOT McKNIGHT, theologian and author

Like most followers of Jesus, I'm very familiar with the Sermon on the Mount. As I opened *Choosing the Opposite*, I wondered if I would find anything new. What a delightful, surprising, challenging, convicting, and ultimately deeply encouraging book! Tammy Melchien writes with the same winsomeness, authenticity, and straight shooting that I experienced with her in person back when we met occasionally for lunch in the Chicago area. Reading this book underscores the basic big-picture truth that our belief in Jesus must lead to simply doing what he says.

NANCY BEACH, leadership coach and coauthor of *Next Sunday*

Tammy Melchien's fresh take on the Sermon on the Mount is a lifeline for anyone tired of culture-war Christianity. She combines her patented deep wisdom with genuine humility on every page. And, as her friend, I've watched her live these truths in the "hidden corners" of her life, which makes her message all the more powerful. If you're looking for a path forward that actually looks like Jesus instead of like our polarized world, this book is for you.

TED CONIARIS, lead pastor of Community Christian Church

Wow, this is such a great read! Tammy is an engaging, funny, and insightful guide to the Sermon on the Mount. While she's clearly read widely and thought deeply, she carries that lightly, resulting in an accessible yet trustworthy companion for this profound section of Scripture. Throughout the book there are regular challenges and invitations to respond, making *Choosing the Opposite* ideal both for groups and individuals.

HANNAH AND ALEX ABSALOM, founders of Dandelion Resourcing

With theological precision, honest grace, and wry humor, Melchien's debut book offers the church a much-needed perspective on what it really means to follow Jesus in our day. Along the way, Melchien pastors the reader, ministering to the longing in our hearts for a different way, a truer home, and intimacy with Christ.

AUBREY SAMPSON, MA, pastor, podcaster, and author of *What We Find in the Dark*, *Big Feelings Days*, and more

Whenever we forget that we were created in his image—and not the other way around—*Choosing the Opposite* serves as a gentle yet powerful reminder of the beauty of our Savior's ways. Tammy's writing invites you into the heart of the biblical narrative, painting vivid scenes that draw you in. Through thought-provoking questions, she encourages deep reflection, making each revelation feel profoundly personal.

NOEMI CHAVEZ, lead pastor of Revive Church

Choosing
THE
Opposite

How the Sermon on the Mount Helps Us Rethink Our Assumptions,

Recalibrate Our Instincts, and Rediscover

THE WAY OF JESUS

Tammy Melchien
FOREWORD BY DAVE FERGUSON

NavPress.com

Choosing the Opposite: How the Sermon on the Mount Helps Us Rethink Our Assumptions, Recalibrate Our Instincts, and Rediscover the Way of Jesus

Copyright © 2025 by Tammy Melchien. All rights reserved.

tammymelchien.com

A NavPress resource published in alliance with Tyndale House Publishers

NavPress is a registered trademark of NavPress, The Navigators, Colorado Springs, CO, registered in the United States of America. The NavPress logo is a trademark of NavPress, The Navigators, Colorado Springs, CO. *Tyndale* is a registered trademark of Tyndale House Ministries, registered in the United States of America. Absence of ® in connection with marks of NavPress or other parties does not indicate an absence of registration of those marks.

The Team:
David Zimmerman, Publisher; Caitlyn Carlson, Senior Editor; Elizabeth Schroll, Copyeditor; Lacie Phillips, Production Assistant; Eva M. Winters, Cover Designer; Cathy Miller, Interior Designer; Sarah Ocenasek, Proofreading Coordinator

Cover and interior illustrations of random arrows copyright © Giovanna/Adobe Stock. All rights reserved.

Author photo copyright © 2024 by Evan Laux. All rights reserved.

All Scripture quotations, unless otherwise indicated, are taken from the Holy Bible, *New International Version*,® *NIV*.® Copyright © 1973, 1978, 1984, 2011 by Biblica, Inc.® Used by permission. All rights reserved worldwide. Scripture quotations marked HCSB are taken from the Holman Christian Standard Bible,® copyright © 1999, 2000, 2002, 2003, 2009 by Holman Bible Publishers. Used by permission. Holman Christian Standard Bible,® Holman CSB,® and HCSB® are federally registered trademarks of Holman Bible Publishers. Scripture quotations marked MSG are taken from *The Message*, copyright © 1993, 2002, 2018 by Eugene H. Peterson. Used by permission of NavPress. All rights reserved. Represented by Tyndale House Publishers. Scripture quotations marked NLT are taken from the *Holy Bible*, New Living Translation, copyright © 1996, 2004, 2015 by Tyndale House Foundation. Used by permission of Tyndale House Publishers, Carol Stream, Illinois 60188. All rights reserved.

Some of the anecdotal illustrations in this book are true to life and are included with the permission of the persons involved. All other illustrations are composites of real situations, and any resemblance to people living or dead is purely coincidental.

For information about special discounts for bulk purchases, please contact Tyndale House Publishers at csresponse@tyndale.com, or call 1-855-277-9400.

ISBN 978-1-64158-934-5

Printed in the United States of America

31	30	29	28	27	26	25
7	6	5	4	3	2	1

For Mom and Dad. Thank you for introducing me to Jesus. And for you, Jesus. You are everything.

Contents

Foreword by Dave Ferguson *xi*

CHAPTER 1 The Opposite *1*
CHAPTER 2 Thinking Upside Down *9*
CHAPTER 3 Choosing Kingdoms *25*
CHAPTER 4 Chasing Grander Dreams *45*
CHAPTER 5 Living the Scriptures *61*
CHAPTER 6 Loving Radically *81*
CHAPTER 7 Performing for the Right Audience *101*
CHAPTER 8 Prioritizing the Kingdom *119*
CHAPTER 9 Growing in Relational Maturity *135*
CHAPTER 10 Hearing and Obeying Jesus *153*

Epilogue *175*
Acknowledgments *179*
Discussion Guide *181*
Notes *197*

Foreword

THERE ARE PEOPLE WHO WRITE BOOKS about following Jesus, and then there are people who live it. Tammy Melchien is one of those rare individuals who does both. I've had the privilege of walking alongside Tammy for over two decades, and from the very beginning, I have known her to be a disciple. Not in the abstract or theoretical sense but in the most practical and powerful way I know how to define it: a disciple is someone who hears from God and does what he says. And over and over, I've watched Tammy do just that—especially when it means choosing the opposite.

When Tammy first joined the staff at COMMUNITY, she had other options. Bigger churches. Better salaries. Clearer paths. In every practical sense, the smart move was to go where the paychecks were large and the resources were plentiful. But Tammy had heard from God, and he had told her to come to COMMUNITY. So she chose the opposite of what culture and instinct would advise. She accepted a part-time role and raised her own support to make it work. That decision didn't just get her on our team—it put her on a trajectory of impact she never could have anticipated.

Later, Tammy heard from God again. This time, he nudged her toward a staff role in Kids' City, our children's ministry. If you know Tammy, you know this wasn't on her radar. She didn't have a passion for children's ministry at the time, and frankly, she wasn't all that interested. But once again, she chose the opposite. She obeyed. And in doing so, she not only became brilliant at developing leaders but also found herself surrounded by peers who would become lifelong friends. That yes shaped her both personally and professionally in profound ways.

The pattern continued when Tammy became a campus pastor and started a new COMMUNITY location in Chicago. It felt daunting. Moving to the city and being a campus pastor was new territory for her. But when God spoke, Tammy listened. She said yes, even when it meant embracing discomfort and uncertainty. And in that season, something beautiful emerged—her teaching gift began to blossom. We started to see a communicator come alive in her, and so did she.

Not long after that, Tammy was offered the role of leading our teaching team—a pioneering move at a time when very few, if any, women across the country were stepping into roles like that. There was no road map. No precedent. Culture assumed this kind of leadership belonged to men. But once again, Tammy chose the opposite. She stepped into that role with humility and strength, and she has been amazing.

Most recently, Tammy made one of her most surprising opposite moves yet. After years of serving on COMMUNITY's directional leadership team—the team with the most authority, decision-making power, and influence—Tammy felt like God was telling her to step down. I tried to talk her out of it. I really did. But she wasn't following me—she was following Jesus. And even when it meant giving up status, control, and visibility, she obeyed. She stepped away from that team to focus on her teaching and writing gifts. And it's in that space that this book was born.

Tammy doesn't just write about choosing the opposite; she lives it. Her life is a case study in what happens when someone says yes to God over and over—especially when it's hard, especially when it costs something, especially when it doesn't make sense. Tammy Melchien is the real deal. And because she is, this book is too.

Choosing the Opposite is a convicting, inspiring, and incredibly well-written book. Tammy doesn't give us a sugarcoated version of faith. She gives us Jesus—the real Jesus. The One who invites us into a counterculturcal Kingdom. The one who challenges our assumptions, flips our instincts upside down, and calls us to live in a way that often goes against the grain of culture and comfort.

With a perceptive look at the Sermon on the Mount, Tammy helps us see how radical and beautiful the way of Jesus really is. She shows us how the opposite way—the way of meekness, mercy, purity, sacrifice, and love—is not weakness but power. Not foolishness but wisdom. Not loss but gain.

You'll find stories in this book that make you smile, truths that make you squirm, and insights that make you think. But more than anything, you'll be given an invitation. Not to admire Jesus from afar but to follow him closely. To be a disciple who hears from God and does what he says—even when it's hard, even when it's opposite of what you would normally do.

My encouragement to you is simple: Don't just read this book. Practice it. Let it mess with you. Let it get in your head and heart and calendar and relationships. Let it shape the way you love, the way you parent, the way you work, the way you vote, and the way you lead. And then—once it's messed with you—pass it on to someone else. Because we don't just need another book on spiritual growth. We need a movement of disciples who are choosing the opposite, one holy step at a time.

If you're serious about following Jesus—not just believing in him but actually living like him—then *Choosing the Opposite* is a must-read. It's timely. It's transformative. I believe it will be the most important book you read this year.

So take a breath. Say a prayer. And get ready to hear from God.

Because the next step he asks you to take may be . . . the opposite.

Dave Ferguson
founding pastor of COMMUNITY and CEO of Exponential

CHAPTER 1

THE OPPOSITE

What if every instinct, every decision you've made up to this point, has led you further from where you really want to be?

What might happen if you did the opposite?

I'M GEN X, AND I'M A TEACHING PASTOR, so if there's a spiritual principle to be gleaned from the classic TV sitcom *Seinfeld*, I'm going to find it. Which is why the more I think about what it's like to follow Jesus, the more I'm reminded of one specific episode.

On the show, most things in life go wrong for lovable loser George Costanza. "My life is the complete opposite of everything I want it to be," he complains. "Every instinct I have, in every aspect of life, be it something to wear, something to eat—it's all been wrong."

So one day he decides to do the opposite of his every instinct. The waitress at Monk's Café asks him if he wants his normal order of tuna on toast, coleslaw, and a cup of coffee, but

George chooses the opposite. He goes for chicken salad on rye, untoasted, with a side of potato salad and a cup of tea.

When Elaine encourages him to approach a woman in the diner, George reminds her, "Bald men with no jobs and no money who live with their parents don't approach strange women!" But Jerry challenges him, "If every instinct you have is wrong, then the opposite would have to be right." So George decides to give it a shot. He approaches the woman, blurts out the truth about his circumstances, and improbably, she becomes his new girlfriend.

As the episode proceeds, George continues to do the opposite of what his natural instincts say. In an interview with the New York Yankees, he shares horrible details about his job experience and insults the team owner to his face. The interviewer muses, "You are the complete opposite of every applicant we've seen," and the owner declares, "Hire this man!"[1]

Okay, you might be thinking, *but* Seinfeld *is meant to be absurdist. After all, it's a show about nothing. This isn't the kind of thing that makes sense in the real world.*

Well, suspend your disbelief for a moment as I suggest something that may seem just as absurd: I'm not sure whether Jesus is a *Seinfeld* fan, but I believe he is calling us to embrace our own George Costanza moment.

What if every instinct, every decision you've made up to this point, has led you further from where you really want to be?

What might happen if you did the opposite?

THE OPPOSITE

Let's face it: It can feel like most things in the world are going wrong. If you care about the future of your community and our world, it's easy to feel anxious, angry, and maybe even a little bit hopeless right now. Culture wars are raging. You're worried that your values are being trampled. You are fearful that if more people don't stand up and do something, the other side will gain even more ground.

If you've been outspoken about your beliefs, chances are a few broken relationships lie in your wake. You no longer trust some people you once cared about. Even if you haven't shared your opinions, you likely feel the damage of this divided and polarized climate deep in your soul. To combat your angst and exhaustion, you've had to mute or block friends and relatives on social media or ditch the platforms altogether.

Everywhere you turn, threats seem to loom on the horizon. Whether it is the instability of the economy, the swift judgment of cancel culture, or the stories of senseless violence filling your newsfeed, life can feel like a precarious journey through a minefield. You long for a sense of security and are vigilant about not letting your guard down.

Maybe you're feeling unnerved by all the rapid changes in our pluralistic society, the relativity and chaos you're seeing around you. You long for a simplicity that will bring a sense of clarity and calm. Or perhaps you feel frustrated that things aren't changing faster. All you see are the hurts and injustices and too many people content to perpetuate them. Nothing is as it should be, and you want to see things change.

No matter where you stand, you sincerely want to follow

Jesus and make a difference in this world—and yet it seems increasingly difficult to do so.

It's easy to look around and see everything going wrong. But I'm going to ask you—and myself—a couple of hard questions: Is it possible we are also playing a role in the disruption and dysfunction? When so much seems to be going sideways, are we just observers, or are we participating in some way? What if we're just as responsible for the problems as the people we blame them on?

> What if every instinct, every decision we've made up to this point, has led us further from where we really want to be?
>
> What might happen if we did the opposite?

Listen, I'm not trying to beat us down, but I am trying to shake us up. I'm writing this as someone who loves the church. I've spent my entire life connected in Christian community, and I've served in ministry for over three decades. I've seen and experienced the beautiful ways that Christ followers have impacted the world. The church can do a tremendous amount of good. But if we're going to be part of disrupting the status quo, we can't just point fingers at "them." We need to consider how many of our choices—the ways you and I and others who follow Jesus have been living—may have contributed to the quagmire we find ourselves in. And I think there is a core reason why we've found ourselves in this spot.

We've wandered down a path where fear and turmoil and

suspicion roil around and within us, where self-protection and a desire for comfort have led us to surround ourselves only with those who think and look and live like us. Understandably, this can seem like the best and safest way to live.

But there is a problem with this path: We can't stay on it and follow Jesus.

Jesus' Kingdom is counterintuitive and radically counter-cultural, and living fully as a citizen in his Kingdom means entering an upside-down kind of life that goes against many of our natural human instincts and regular patterns of being. When Jesus invites us into the Kingdom of God, he's calling us to an opposite kind of life.

And too many of us aren't living it.

We know we aren't flourishing, but we have no idea why. The world feels complicated and scary, and our relationships can be painful and tense, but we don't know how to make things right. Too many of us aren't experiencing the life Jesus offers us because the gospel we've embraced is not the Good News of the Kingdom. Without realizing it, we're practicing a faith often more informed by inherited assumptions, cultural influences, and political ideology than by the teachings of Jesus.

The late philosopher Dallas Willard notes,

> What we are looking at in the contemporary Western world is precisely what [Jesus] himself foretold. We *have* heard him. For almost two millennia we have heard him. . . . But we have chosen to not do what he said. He warned that this would make us "like a silly

man who built his house on a sand foundation. The rain poured down, and the rivers and winds beat upon that house, and it collapsed into total disaster" (Matt. 7:26-27). We today stand in the midst of precisely the disaster he foretold.[2]

HEAR FROM GOD

Do you realize that God wants to speak to you? If you are a follower of Jesus, God is present with you and within you through the Holy Spirit. How absurd to think he would be that near to you and not have anything to say! And yet many of us go about our daily lives without expecting to hear from him.

Throughout this book, I am going to encourage you to pause and give God opportunities to communicate with you. We're going to be digging into Scripture, and God always speaks through his Word. God often uses other people to communicate with us, so there may be something in my writing that God wants to use to speak to you. But I believe God also wants to speak to you through your own thoughts, emotions, and spirit. I encourage you to pause from time to time to pay attention to him. When you become aware of something stirring within you—whether it be a new idea, a feeling of discomfort or anger, or just a fuzzy notion that you should be paying attention—stop and ask the Spirit to open your mind and heart to receive and understand what God is saying to you. Pray: *Lord, I want to hear from you. Come, Holy Spirit. Speak to me and empower me to do what you say. Amen.*

Two thousand years ago, Jesus showed up on the shores of the Sea of Galilee and began teaching a group of people a new way to live. He invited them into a Kingdom that was different from anything they'd ever experienced or known. To live in this Kingdom often required that they do the opposite of their naturally formed instincts. It requires the same of us today.

Let's stop settling for everything going wrong and instead look at our natural impulses and where they've gotten us. I consider myself somewhat of an expert on blowing it, and I'm happy to share what I've learned the hard way. But I'm not just going to speak to you from my own experience. Jesus' most famous collection of teachings, the Sermon on the Mount, tells us a lot about the opposite kind of life. This "manifesto . . . for the life of the individual follower of Christ in the midst of the community of his followers"[3] very well might be *the* most important passage of Scripture for Christ followers living in this current moment.

The Sermon holds the wisdom we need to find a better way forward, but here's what we need to know up front: We're not going to like a lot of it. At times, Jesus is going to rub us the wrong way. We like the idea of being saved from our sins; we don't want to love our enemies.

And yet, if enough people decided to actually follow him, we'd turn the world upside down. After all, it's happened before.

I believe doing the opposite could help create peace in your community. The counterintuitive way of Jesus could help you mend relationships without compromising what you believe. It could bring healing to the rifts with family and friends that grieve you.

I believe doing the opposite could also bring calm to your own soul. Instead of living riddled with fear or anxiety or anger over what is happening in our world, you could live with a quiet confidence that Jesus is on his throne and the Kingdom is not shaken. You could let go of feeling responsible for burdens that are not yours to bear. You can experience the lived reality of *the Son setting you free*.[4]

And I believe doing the opposite could bring healing to our world. If we, as followers of Jesus, do the opposite of what our natural instincts say, of the impulses that often bring us to these moments of division and distrust, we could restore our credibility to the watching world. We could make the difference we long to make. We could help people find their way back to God and together bring more of his Kingdom to earth.

I really do believe there is a hopeful way forward.

If we're willing to listen to Jesus.

If we leave behind what isn't working and take a risk together, we'll discover that Jesus is about to turn everything upside down.

CHAPTER 2

THINKING UPSIDE DOWN

Matthew 5:1-12

IMAGINE YOU'RE SITTING on a gently sloping hillside, looking out over a panoramic view of the Sea of Galilee. It's warm. The humidity is making your clothing sticky. You squint as the sun beats down on your sweaty forehead. There are hundreds of people milling around, maybe even thousands. All of you have come to see this new rabbi everyone is talking about, the one who has been announcing a new Kingdom. You're not sure where all this will go. You feel a bit concerned that the situation could get violent. This rabbi seems to be talking of revolution—and Rome's Caesar won't like that. Caesar holds all the power, and his minions are never far away.

But you are desperate for hope, and so you are here. Wondering. Waiting. Weary.

The crowd begins to stir, and someone makes shushing noises. You don't know what is happening. But then, as everyone settles down, you see him: Jesus. He sits down. The rabbi is about to teach.

When I imagine this scene, I see a whole collection of ordinary people sitting on that hillside, anxious to hear what Jesus has to say. I picture him looking into the eyes of a disheveled man sitting just to his left, a day laborer who always wonders where his next meal will come from. He hasn't had a bath in weeks. In the synagogue, no one ever rises to greet him. It's not that anyone treats him badly; it's more like they don't even notice he's there. He's considered a nobody. But Jesus looks at him, and with a sparkle in his eye, says,

> "Blessed are the poor in spirit,
> for theirs is the kingdom of heaven."
> MATTHEW 5:3

A noise to his right draws Jesus' gaze. A toddler tugs on his mother's head covering, trying to get her attention. As the boy settles into the woman's lap, she looks up to see Jesus staring in her direction. Tears immediately begin to well up in her eyes. Somehow she knows that he knows. There is something in his expression that tells her that Jesus is aware of her grief, of what she has lost. Tenderly he says,

> "Blessed are those who mourn,
> for they will be comforted."
> MATTHEW 5:4

A few moments later, his eyes fall on a struggling shopkeeper. This man is well liked by everyone, especially those who are struggling. Almost everyone in his village and the two down the road can tell a story of how he was kind to them at a time when they were in need. His peers like him too, although at times they mock his poor business sense. They think it is ridiculous that sometimes he can barely clothe his own children but will give away a bag of grain to someone he doesn't even know. His business could be booming, but his tender heart always gets in the way. Jesus smiles at this man and says,

> "Blessed are the merciful,
> for they will be shown mercy."
> MATTHEW 5:7

As you take all this in on that hillside in Galilee, it leaves your head spinning. None of these blessings make any sense. And yet you find yourself drawn to this strange rabbi. His words give you hope you never thought possible.

Upside-Down Blessings

Jesus begins the Sermon on the Mount with blessings. Right away, these blessings, which we know as the Beatitudes, are training his followers to think differently about what life in the Kingdom of God looks like. Jesus knows that much of his Kingdom vision will be the opposite of how people have been culturally conditioned to think. New Testament scholar Warren Carter writes,

In the beatitudes, Jesus has the disciples imagine a different world, a different identity for themselves, a different set of practices, a different relationship to the status quo. Why imagine? Not because it is impossible. Not because it is escapist. Not because it is fantasy. But because it begins to counter patterns imbibed from the culture of the imperial world.[1]

We often misread the Beatitudes as a list of virtues we should try to cultivate in our lives. We think Jesus wants us to figure out how to be meek, to hunger and thirst for righteousness, to be a peacemaker. We're never quite sure how we're supposed to become poor or persecuted. But the Beatitudes aren't statements telling us what to do; they are observations of what is. Jesus is looking into the faces of worn-out and weary people sitting on a hillside and announcing to them: "Wherever you find yourself, whatever you are going through, you are blessed!"

The Beatitudes are good news!

And they are absurd. Because Jesus is calling *blessed* people whom no one else would have called blessed.

Everyone knows the rich have it made, but Jesus says the poor are blessed.

It seems obvious that the assertive get their way, but Jesus says the meek are blessed.

Most everyone values comfort and security, but Jesus says the persecuted are blessed.

Jesus is looking into the faces of so-called nobodies. Likely some in the crowd don't have a cent to their name. Some carry the shame of the horrible mistakes they've made. Others have been labeled and cast aside to the outskirts of society. Chances are good that none of them *feel* blessed.

And yet Jesus says, "You are blessed!"

Through the Beatitudes, Jesus is inviting us to radically shift our perspective.

Perspective can make all the difference. We've all probably lived through situations or circumstances that were difficult, painful even. If we only see them through that lens, we can find ourselves living wounded, wary, or bitter, even years after. But what if we shift our perspective to look for what God was doing *in us* in those seasons? We still would never have wished to go through them, but we can discover a strange gratitude for what came from them.

I'm reminded of the season I spent doing ministry in a small college town in central Illinois. While I loved caring for the college students there, I had no peer community of my own. Evenings and weekends were solitary. I often felt empty. However, this time of intense loneliness became one of the most important seasons in my life. Because I had no one else to spend time with, I learned to spend my days communing with Jesus. It was not unusual for me to spend hours at a time in prayer and Bible study and journaling. This wasn't because I'm more spiritual than other people; it was because I literally had nothing else to do! Don't misunderstand me—I don't value loneliness. Difficult circumstances are and will always be painful. Yet if we change our perspective, we may be able to discover unexpected blessings in the middle of them.

Through the Beatitudes, Jesus is asking his listeners to make a seismic shift in their perspective. Up to this point, they've likely seen themselves as stuck in the shadows of life. They don't have power. They aren't wealthy. They are struggling. Some are suffering. And yet here is Jesus, seated before them, telling them they are looking at their situations all wrong.

In his Kingdom, they are the blessed ones!

It's absurd.

And yet it's true.

They are blessed because the source of all true blessing is inviting them to follow him into a Kingdom that doesn't operate like the kingdoms they've known. Theologian Jonathan Pennington writes, "Jesus is offering and inviting his hearers into *the way of being in the world that will result in their true and full flourishing now and in the age to come.*"[2]

Through the Beatitudes, Jesus is inviting you to experience life with him in the Kingdom of God, to view yourself through his eyes instead of through the lens of what you've always thought mattered. When you choose a way of life that's the opposite of how most people are living, you will discover something extraordinary: intimacy with God and genuine community with others.

And yet that's when an unwanted reality smacks you in the face.

For as you sit there on that hillside listening to Jesus pronounce these blessings, you turn to your left and then to your right. You notice the tax collector who bullied and cheated you. You catch a glimpse of the religious leader who judged you. You spot the neighbor who exhausts and irritates you. You see the prostitute whose shame disgusts you. You recognize the Zealot whose politics terrify you. And you realize that Jesus is also pronouncing these blessings on the people who bother you. This blessing is for everyone.

Let's be honest. Most of us would rather Jesus didn't bless *that person* or *that group of people*. We might never admit that aloud, but deep down, it's how we feel.

This is why the Beatitudes are so countercultural. If you're going to fully embrace the truth of these blessings, the most radical shift in perspective isn't in how you think about yourself. It's in confronting the reality that there are people in your life and community whom you don't want to see blessed—and that Jesus is going to bless them anyway.

No Blessing for You!

I was canoeing down a river when I discovered I had, in fact, made my own determinations about whom I thought God should bless. In the back of the boat sat a woman who had become an influential mentor in my life. She didn't just profess belief in Jesus—I'd watched her live out that faith in practical ways. Her impact on my own journey of discipleship had been so significant that after I'd graduated college, I'd moved across the country for a ministry internship under her supervision.

As we floated down the lazy river with several dozen college students, somehow the topic of politics came up. That's when I heard my mentor say, "Yeah, I typically vote Democrat"—and I froze midpaddle.

Now, you should know that I grew up in a wonderful Christian family and church that nurtured in me a love for

Jesus and the desire to follow him. But one of the things I internalized from my family and church culture was that American Christians voted Republican. I don't think anyone ever taught me this directly, but I had certainly absorbed this view from the atmosphere around me. I wasn't even fully aware of it until this moment, when I, at age twenty-two, heard a committed Christ follower I respected contradict a belief I'd taken for granted.

It's probably good that I was in the front of the boat so she didn't see the look on my face. *How can this be?* I was stunned. I had no mental framework for this: that a person could be a follower of Jesus—never mind someone whose life reflected God's ways more than anyone else I'd ever met—and yet be a Democrat.

Maybe some of you can relate and right now you're ready to put down this book because the whole idea of a Christian who votes for a Democrat seems at best like an oxymoron and at worst like blasphemy. Or if you had a different political upbringing than I did, you might feel the same way about Republicans.

It makes me wonder if we'd be offended by the sorts of people Jesus invited into his Kingdom.

Many of us have adopted a misguided notion that it is our job as Christians to measure other people against a list of protocols that determine whether someone is acceptable and worthy of blessing.

Don't vote the way I think you should? No blessing for you!

Don't side with me on that culture-war issue? No blessing for you!

Don't translate a verse in 1 Timothy the way I translate it? No blessing for you!

Don't hold the same beliefs about sexuality that I hold? No blessing for you!

Don't belong to my circle? No blessing for you!

If I may gently challenge you: That way of thinking is not in line with the way of Jesus.

The people who annoy and offend us—politically, culturally, even doctrinally—are the sorts of people Jesus invites into his Kingdom.

Sure, there aren't any Democrats or Republicans sitting on that hillside in Galilee, but there are Herodians and Pharisees and Sadducees and Zealots. Many of the women and men in front of Jesus this day hold all sorts of twisted ideas about power and politics and religion. They are caught up in all types of sinful behavior and relational dysfunction. They are just like you and me. And they are just like the people who bother us.

And yet Jesus does not bring a word of condemnation or separation. He brings an invitation: Blessing for everyone!

With his absurd, upside-down blessings ringing out on that hillside in Galilee, Jesus looks over the crowd seated before him. These are the ones the Father is giving to him.[3] He knows they don't realize it yet, but seated before him is a new family, a new community, his Kingdom community. He pauses, taking it all in, and then speaks another blessing:

> "Blessed are the peacemakers,
> for they will be called children of God."
> MATTHEW 5:9

In a world rife with division, these men and women and boys and girls are the ones who will help him bring peace. But the way before them will be hard. Some people will misunderstand them. Others will openly oppose them. Sometimes—and maybe often—misunderstanding and opposition will come from fellow Jesus followers. After all, when you set out to dismantle the kingdoms of this world, forces seen and unseen will try to stop you, to create division, to sow distrust.

Jesus leans forward, almost as if sharing a secret, and says,

> "Blessed are those who are persecuted because of
>   righteousness,
>   for theirs is the kingdom of heaven.
>
> "Blessed are you when people insult you, persecute you and falsely say all kinds of evil against you because of me."
> **MATTHEW 5:10-11**

Blessed. Blessed. Blessed. Jesus knows that his words won't make sense to them yet, but he also knows they will need to remember them. Because although this journey won't be easy, the Kingdom way of life is the path to freedom and flourishing.

The Opposite

If we're going to follow Jesus in the way of his Kingdom, we have to let him turn our thinking upside down—to open us up to a new perspective. As we go on this journey through his Sermon together, we'll likely have moments when Jesus' teaching feels uncomfortable, disruptive, perhaps even offensive. In these moments, let's pause and ask ourselves, *What if this instinct, this way I tend to respond in moments like these, hasn't led to my life or relationships or community looking more like the Kingdom of God? What would the opposite of this reaction look like?*

Let me be clear: I'm not saying that to follow Jesus we should abandon all our gut instincts, but I do think we need to be willing to examine and challenge them. We have to pay attention to our regular ways of thinking and acting and reacting and consider whether the outcomes look like the kind of life, the kinds of flourishing relationships and communities, that Jesus is offering. Because if not, then we have to consider the possibility that it is not Jesus' teaching we are following but, in the words of Warren Carter, "patterns imbibed from the culture of the imperial world."[4]

In his letter to the Romans, the apostle Paul writes,

> Do not conform to the pattern of this world, but *be transformed by the renewing of your mind.* Then you will be able to test and approve what God's will is— his good, pleasing and perfect will.
>
> **ROMANS 12:2** (EMPHASIS MINE)

It's human nature. By default, we conform to the patterns around us. And because we live in a broken world that is still steeped in sin, this can remain true even *after* we come to believe in Jesus. Without intention and effort, our ways of thinking can remain unexamined, unchallenged, and unchanged, and we will never get to experience the fullness of life in God's Kingdom. New Testament scholar N. T. Wright points out, "Many Christians in today's world never come to terms with this. They hope they will be able to live up to something like Christian standards while still thinking the way the rest of the world thinks. It can't be done."[5] If we don't take the time to step back in solitude and silence to partner with the Holy Spirit in examining our thoughts, attitudes, and values, we will miss out on the transformation that God desires to bring in our lives.

And yet the good news is that as we engage in this practice of renewing our minds, we will open ourselves to the Spirit's work of transformation. We'll grow in wisdom and understanding of Jesus' ways. And our gut instincts will begin to align more and more with his Kingdom so that we will be able to "test and approve what God's will is" (Romans 12:2) in the circumstances and situations we find ourselves in.

That day in the canoe, when my ingrained beliefs about politics and faith revealed I'd made assumptions and judgment calls about how a Christian was required to vote, I had a choice to make. I could cling to my long-held ways of thinking and decide that anyone who disagrees with me deserves to be shunned, shamed, or perhaps even cursed. Or I could choose to see such a person as someone Jesus wants me to bless. I could lay my regular patterns of thinking before God and let him transform my mind so that I could begin to see politics not through a partisan lens but through a Kingdom lens.

Admittedly, that Kingdom lens has made voting a much

more difficult task for me. It's much easier to just pick a political camp and see everything as black-and-white, good or bad, right or wrong. But where has that way of operating, which characterizes so much of the American political landscape today, gotten us? Do our churches, our communities, our relationships look more like God's Kingdom when we dig our political trenches and lob curses at one another instead of blessings?

I want to be a Kingdom-minded person. Now whenever I vote, I wrestle through every decision with Jesus. I want to vote on each candidate and issue the way I think Jesus would vote if he were me, and I no longer believe that can happen down party lines. So I set aside the *R*s and *D*s and ask the Holy Spirit to guide my understanding. I filter each candidate and issue through what I know of God's heart for the world and his care for every single one of his image bearers. I'm sure I don't get every voting decision right, but my goal isn't to get it right. My goal is to try as best I can to think and act like Jesus. My goal is to live as a citizen of the Kingdom of God—and to join Jesus in bringing that Kingdom however I can, right where I am.

The cultural sea we swim in teaches us to label, exclude, and condemn people who are different from us, instincts that are running rampant not just in the world but also in the church. At the very beginning of the Sermon, Jesus confronts this pattern: the subconscious belief that it is our job to decide who is worthy or unworthy of blessing, who is in and who is out.

This is not the way of Jesus.

Jesus embodied the opposite. When he looked into a face, he saw a person made in his image and extended a blessing. He wasn't interested in keeping people out; he invited everyone in.

Of course, God gave them the same free will he gives us, the ability to choose to follow him or not. But the door was always wide open to them. It still is.

Doing the opposite means looking into the face of a person who holds different beliefs than you do, who votes differently than you do, who is part of a different tribe than you are, and saying, "I want blessing for you." And—here is the hard part—*you have to really mean it.*

Let's be honest. Most of us aren't there yet. I know I'm not. But I want to be. And I know I won't be able to live this opposite kind of life unless I let God transform my mind and heart.

HEAR FROM GOD

Lord, I want to hear from you. Come, Holy Spirit. Speak to me and empower me to do what you say. Amen.

We all absorb ways of thinking from the culture around us. These thoughts shape how we view people, especially people who are different from us. Quiet yourself before God. Ask him to bring to your mind a person or group of people you don't want to see blessed. Try not to get defensive or rationalize. Just hear what God wants to say to you.

What did God say to you? What will you do in response?

Being transformed by the renewing of your mind requires humility, curiosity, and teachability. If we are going to learn to think and act like God's Kingdom people, we must have the humility to admit we were wrong and accept that we'll be wrong again. We need to be curious, not defensive, when confronted with information or opinions that contradict our own. Rather than digging in our heels to defend our positions, we ask questions. We wrestle with points of view we've never considered. As we open ourselves to the Spirit of truth, who wants to guide us to truth, we become teachable. We learn. And as we live this way, we increasingly find ourselves transformed into people whose first instinct is formed not by our culture but instead by the way of Christ.

Jesus' Kingdom way will often leave us asking, like the crowds gathered around him in John 6, "This is a hard teaching. Who can accept it?"[6] Following Jesus in the ways of his Kingdom requires letting go of many things that seem justified according to our former way of thinking. It often feels like we're losing more than winning.[7] Many of the people in Jesus' orbit couldn't fathom that kind of opposite life: "From this time many of his disciples turned back and no longer followed him."[8] The same thing happens today. Sometimes people reject Jesus outright, but more often they opt for believing in him but not really following him.

If you aren't paying attention, it could even happen to you.

The twelve disciples chose a different path though. When Jesus asked if they wanted to leave too, Peter spoke up for the group:

> "Lord, to whom shall we go? You have the words of eternal life. We have come to believe and to know that you are the Holy One of God."
>
> JOHN 6:68-69

The Twelve declared their allegiance to Jesus, and then they followed him beyond belief and did what he told them to do as they lived their lives in the Kingdom of God. What will we do?

CHAPTER 3

CHOOSING KINGDOMS

Matthew 4:17

FLYING ACROSS TIME ZONES can be difficult. I've stared in awe at the Pantheon in Rome, struggled to catch my breath on the rim of the Grand Canyon, and openly cried as I've traced Jesus' footsteps to the cross on the Via Dolorosa in Jerusalem. I consider myself very fortunate to have had those experiences. And yet traveling long distances also comes with a significant downside: jet lag.

Jet lag is that disorienting experience when your body, attuned to one time zone, suddenly has to exist hours ahead of or behind itself. Your brain, nervous system, and sleep rhythms all think you're in Chicago, but you're actually in Frankfurt, Germany. And you are caught in between.

home country YOU international country

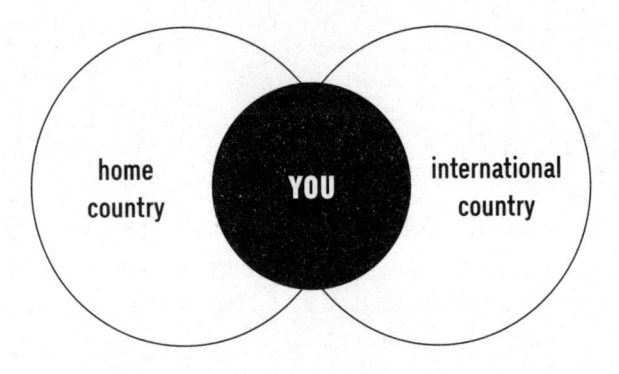

The last time I traveled overseas, jet lag hit me hard. During the day I felt sluggish and dazed. As I tried to engage with my surroundings, I found myself pulled—controlled, even—by the old reality of Chicago time. Overnight I kept waking up at 1:00 a.m., ready for adventure, and then had to lie quietly in bed for hours so I wouldn't disturb everyone else in the house.

Any seasoned traveler will tell you that the best way to overcome jet lag is to immediately and completely adapt to your new reality. The minute you sit down on the plane, adjust your watch to your destination's time and switch your eating habits to the new location's rhythms. You need to force your body to rest even when it doesn't feel tired and push yourself to stay awake even when you feel drowsy. If you do this, the experts say, your body rhythms will more quickly adjust to the new time zone.

Here's what I've realized: The upside-down, counterintuitive way of Jesus creates a similar disorientation, a spiritual jet lag that we experience when we decide to follow him. We move from the reality we've been living in to a different reality, and the adjustment is difficult. We often feel ourselves pulled, controlled even, by our old reality even though we want to live in the new. We haven't changed time zones—we've changed kingdoms.

When Jesus came into our world and began to teach people, he was clear about his goal: to invite us into his Kingdom, showing us what it looks like to move from our old reality into a new one. Heaven, Jesus announced, was breaking through to earth:

> "Repent, for the kingdom of heaven has come near."
> MATTHEW 4:17

When Jesus says that the Kingdom of Heaven or the Kingdom of God[1] *has come near*, he's telling us that when he arrived on earth, he brought the Kingdom with him. God chose to become a human and walk among us, opening an opportunity for a new way, a better way of living in this world: as part of his Kingdom. And Jesus went around teaching people how to experience it.

If we are going to follow Jesus, it is important that we understand the nature of this Kingdom, yet I have found that most Christians can't tell you what the Kingdom of God is, let alone how to live in it. That's why the Sermon on the Mount—considered the best collection of Jesus' teachings explaining Kingdom life—is so important. New Testament professor Amy-Jill Levine writes,

> These three chapters tell us that the kingdom of
> heaven is not some abstract place with pearly gates and
> golden slippers, harp music, and a bunch of angels

flapping their wings. The kingdom of heaven occurs when people take the words of Jesus in these chapters to heart and live into them.[2]

So before we move forward, let's make sure we understand this focal point of Jesus' teaching—what it looks like to adjust our rhythms, our choices, our whole way of being to our new reality. What exactly *is* the Kingdom of God?

The Kingdom and the Kingdoms

Kingdom of God

The Kingdom of God is like a sphere—an all-encompassing space in which God's will reigns. Here's how Dallas Willard defines the Kingdom:

> God's own "kingdom," or "rule," is the range of his effective will, where what he wants done is done. The person of God himself and the action of his will are the organizing principles of his kingdom, but everything that obeys those principles, whether by nature or by choice, is *within* his kingdom.[3]

The Kingdom is what reality looks like when God's dream and intention for life are being lived out among his people. Did you know God has a dream for your life? He always has. He wants you to experience shalom. *Shalom* is the biblical word for peace, but as theologian Cornelius Plantinga Jr. explains,

> it means far more than mere peace of mind or a ceasefire between enemies. In the Bible, shalom means *universal flourishing, wholeness, and delight*—a rich state of affairs in which natural needs are satisfied and natural gifts fruitfully employed, a state of affairs that inspires joyful wonder as its Creator and Savior opens doors and welcomes the creatures in whom he delights. Shalom, in other words, is the way things ought to be.[4]

Did you catch that? Simply put: "Shalom . . . is the way things ought to be."

In this shalom, God wants you to experience deep intimacy with him and mutually fulfilling relationships with others. He wants you to have a sense of well-being in the deepest parts of your soul. He wants you to know the joy of living for a purpose bigger than yourself. Bottom line: God wants you to flourish!

Now, flourishing doesn't mean that God is necessarily all that concerned with what job you have or your income bracket or your status in society. Nor does flourishing mean that you are immune from struggles or suffering. Your experience of shalom isn't dependent on your material realities. The life God has for you exists outside and above financial security and circumstantial stability. Wherever you find yourself, God wants you to experience "life . . . to the full"[5]—the kind of life that can only be found in his Kingdom.

God rules as King over his Kingdom. But how are we to think of God as King? What does his reign look like? If our only concept of a king comes from what we've read in classic novels or British tabloid magazines, we need to understand that God's kingship looks like, well, the opposite of all that. Jesus hints at this when he teaches his disciples:

> "You know that the rulers of the Gentiles lord it over them, and their high officials exercise authority over them. Not so with you. Instead, whoever wants to become great among you must be your servant, and whoever wants to be first must be your slave—just as the Son of Man did not come to be served, but to serve, and to give his life as a ransom for many."
> MATTHEW 20:25-28

Do you want to know how God rules? Look at Jesus. God is not domineering or authoritarian or distant or uncaring. He came among us as One who serves. He is the King who describes himself as "gentle and humble in heart."[6]

God as King is more like a good, healthy parent. Good parents sacrifice for their children. Good parents seek to be gentle even in correction. Good parents want their kids to be happy and whole. A good parent doesn't want to dictate all the choices their child makes, but parents do have a pretty good idea which decisions will help their children flourish and which will lead their children down a more difficult, often painful path.

God is a perfect parent who wants all his children to flourish. So he came to earth in the person of Jesus to embody and teach us his way of human flourishing—of living in the sphere in which what he wants done is done.

The Kingdom of God is a present reality because Jesus brought it near, but it is not a completed reality. Obviously, God's will is not done everywhere. This is often described as the "now and not yet" of the Kingdom. The Kingdom is here now, but it isn't fully realized. That's why Jesus taught us to pray:

> "Your kingdom come,
> your will be done,
> on earth as it is in heaven."
>
> MATTHEW 6:10

We are to pray for God to bring more of his Kingdom to earth. But we're not just to pray; we're also meant to be an answer to those prayers as we join God in bringing more of his Kingdom to earth.

- When we share the Good News of Jesus with a neighbor or friend, we are joining God in bringing more of his Kingdom to earth.

- When we help the poor and vulnerable living among us, we are joining God in bringing more of his Kingdom to earth.

- When we act as peacemakers in the middle of relational strife, we are joining God in bringing more of his Kingdom to earth.

- When we stand against injustice in our neighborhoods and cities, we are joining God in bringing more of his Kingdom to earth.

Whenever we do the will of God, we are living in the Kingdom and helping bring more of it to earth.

When Jesus returns, the Kingdom will be fully restored. In the new heaven and new earth, we will experience life as God always intended it to be. With God's will reigning everywhere, "there will be no more death or mourning or crying or pain."[7]

But for now, other kingdoms remain.

What are these kingdoms? The kingdoms of the world.

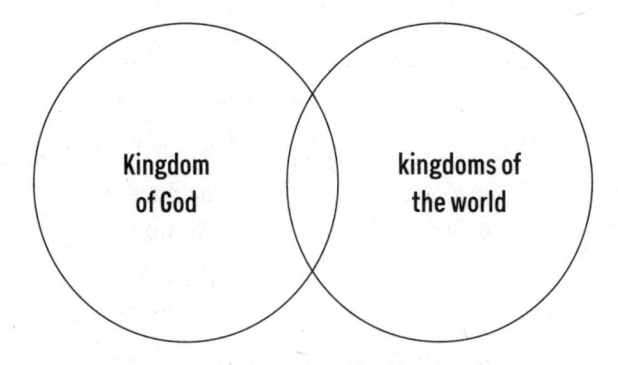

Kingdom of God | kingdoms of the world

Author John Ortberg describes them this way:

> On earth, all our little kingdoms intersect and merge and form larger kingdoms—families, corporations,

nations, and economic, political, and cultural systems. We could call that whole conglomeration the "kingdom of the earth." And that kingdom is junked up by sin.[8]

In practical terms, this means that all our human systems are kingdoms of this world.

Amazon and Apple and all other businesses and corporations are kingdoms of this world.

Wall Street, capitalism, and our banking systems are kingdoms of this world.

Fox News, MSNBC, CNN, social media, and all the other media empires are kingdoms of this world.

The Republican Party is a kingdom of this world.

The Democratic Party is a kingdom of this world.

The United States and Russia and Israel and all modern nation-states are kingdoms of this world.

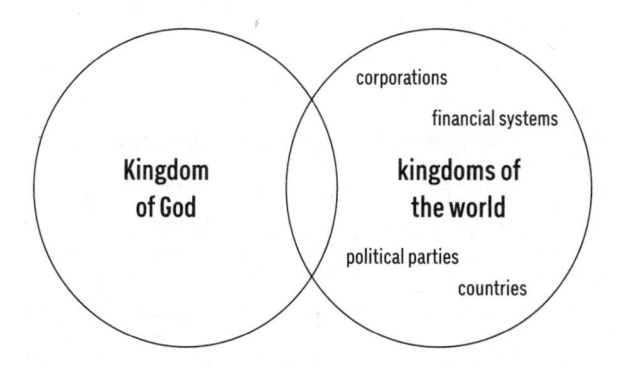

Venn diagram showing two overlapping circles labeled "Kingdom of God" and "kingdoms of the world", with "corporations", "financial systems", "political parties", and "countries" listed in the kingdoms of the world circle.

Do you see the overlap in these circles? That's because at times some beliefs and practices in each of these kingdoms do conform to God's will. But in each of these kingdoms, there will always be beliefs and practices that stand in opposition to the Kingdom of God.

It is critical that followers of Jesus recognize this! As Ortberg says, these kingdoms of the earth are "junked up by sin." Only one kingdom is fully in alignment with the heart and will of God, and that is the Kingdom of God.

So let's ask ourselves some hard questions:

- Which kingdoms of this world do we find ourselves attached to?
- Which kingdoms do we tend to uncritically align ourselves with?
- What do our actions and words and motives reveal about our kingdom alliances?

We need to grapple with the reality that it is possible to claim the name of Jesus but continue to live aligned with the kingdoms of this world. Pastor Tara Beth Leach warns,

> It's possible to believe in Jesus and not have Jesus driving our lives.
> It's possible to believe in Jesus and live in a way that is counter to the kingdom of God.
> It's possible to believe in Jesus and live nothing like Jesus.
> It's possible to believe in Jesus and live as citizens of this world instead of the kingdom.[9]

If we're not paying attention, if we're not intentionally holding our lives up to Jesus' teachings about the Kingdom, we can easily find ourselves adopting the values and practices of the kingdoms of this world.

- Jesus taught about humble service,[10] but too many Christians see power as the solution to their problems.
- Jesus taught about holding on to the truth,[11] but too many Christians are comfortable embracing half-truths and unfounded rumors if they serve a desired agenda.
- Jesus taught a message of peace,[12] but too many Christians believe military might is the way to solve the world's conflicts.
- Jesus taught about confident hope,[13] but too many Christians live terrified of the future.
- Jesus taught a practice of enemy love,[14] but too many Christians want to see their enemies shamed, punished, and destroyed.

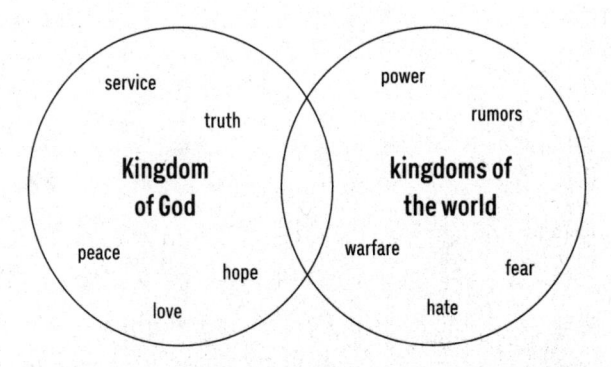

I can feel the pull to align with the kingdoms of this world. Do you?

Jesus told us not to fear,[15] yet we continue to tune in to our favorite cable news commentators, who strategically use fear tactics—tactics that are effective at boosting their ratings and revenues—while convincing us to demonize the other side.

Jesus told us that our heavenly Father cares for the birds of the air and considers us "much more valuable than they,"[16] yet our emotions rise and fall with the green or red numbers on Wall Street.

Jesus told us to expect the world to hate us,[17] yet we are drawn to cultural and theological positions that will earn us social media clicks and the applause of popular people.

Jesus told us not to put our trust in weapons,[18] yet we often do, believing that our right to protect ourselves with guns should be prioritized against any attempt to put boundaries around those weapons, despite the risk they pose to fellow image bearers.

Jesus told us that his victory would be won by going to the cross,[19] yet we often speak and act as though in order for his Kingdom to advance on this earth, we have to get our preferred candidates in the White House and the halls of Congress.

The kingdoms of the world still have a lot of pull over us, and the ruler of these kingdoms wants to distract us, confuse us, and deceive us into thinking our preferred lesser kingdom is the same as God's Kingdom. But we don't have to fall for the devil's lies. When Jesus brought the Kingdom near, he broke the power of the evil one and empowered us to walk away from lesser kingdoms. The apostle Paul reminds us,

> As for you, you were dead in your transgressions and sins, in which you used to live when you followed the ways of this world and of the ruler of the kingdom of

the air, the spirit who is now at work in those who are disobedient.

EPHESIANS 2:1-2

In other words, Paul is saying, "You used to live that way, but no more!" To the Colossians he adds, "He has rescued us from the dominion of darkness and brought us into the kingdom of the Son he loves, in whom we have redemption, the forgiveness of sins."[20]

We have been welcomed into the only kingdom worth living for! The beauty and hope of the Kingdom of God help us see lesser kingdoms for what they really are. But here's the reality: *We must choose.* In every moment of every day, we get to choose which kingdom we'll align ourselves with.

For we, too, have kingdoms. Every person has a kingdom. I have a kingdom, and you have a kingdom. My kingdom is the little sphere in which I get to call the shots. Your kingdom is the little sphere in which what you say goes. Our personal kingdoms are where we decide whether to align with lesser kingdoms or join the Kingdom of God.

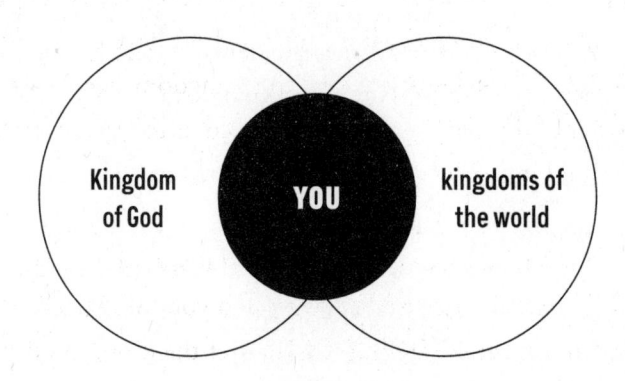

Kingdom of God — YOU — kingdoms of the world

Understand this: God gave us our kingdoms. They are a good thing—part of what it means to be made in his image.[21] God created us with the freedom to make choices. As a perfect parent—and as the King over all creation—he knows which choices will lead to shalom; but as a good Father, as a benevolent King, he gives us the agency to decide for ourselves.

Other kingdoms will always pull at us because that's where our human selves naturally want to go—toward tangible security, comfort, and control. But entering the Kingdom of God means consistently choosing the opposite.

Jesus describes that decision this way: "*Repent*, for the kingdom of heaven has come near."[22]

The Opposite

Most of us hear the word *repent* and think of feeling sorry or regretful. Maybe we picture having to grovel or sulk in shame. But that's not what repentance is. Repentance isn't centered on feelings.

In the original language of the New Testament, Greek, the word for *repent* means "to change one's mind."[23] Repentance involves rethinking your entire view of reality, and not just as an intellectual exercise. As New Testament scholar N. T. Wright puts it:

> [*repent*] means "change direction"; "turn round and go the other way"; or "stop what you're doing and do the opposite instead." How you *feel* about it isn't the really important thing. It's what you *do* that matters.[24]

Did you catch that? Repentance is about doing *the opposite*. Repentance is directional. Let's say you are traveling on the interstate en route to an amazing vacation destination—when suddenly you realize you're driving in the wrong direction. What do you do? You immediately start looking for an exit. You want to turn around and head in the right direction. If you don't, you're just going to get more and more off track and miss the good thing you're longing for!

When Jesus calls us to *repent*, it's an invitation to take the exit ramp so that we can turn around and start heading the opposite way.

And yet many people choose to fly right by the exit. Maybe even many of us. We continue down the road we've been traveling because we've convinced ourselves that it's actually the right way—when in reality the destination is far from where Jesus calls us to be. Or we've just set the cruise control and are mindlessly moving through life without giving much thought to where we are going. We follow the roads we've always known, never really questioning whether they are leading us in the way of Jesus. Repentance is an intentional choice to notice where we are, to be honest with ourselves about where we've been heading, and to change direction. Repentance is necessary if we are going to begin living in the Kingdom of God.

Repentance is directional, and it is also demonstrative. It requires action.

To better understand what Jesus means by this word, it can be helpful to see how it was used in contexts outside the Bible in the first century. Josephus, a well-known first-century historian and military leader, writes of an incident around AD 66 where repentance played a key role. Josephus discovered that a bandit had plotted to kill him, and after Josephus foiled the plan, he told the man that he would overlook the offense if the bandit showed repentance. In the context of Josephus's words, this repentance was not about the bandit feeling sorry or groveling; it was about him proving that he had changed his mind, had abandoned his treacherous agenda, and was committed to being loyal to Josephus. The bandit would have to demonstrate his repentance with action: sticking by Josephus's side, fighting alongside Josephus in battles, and following Josephus's orders.[25]

Repentance is demonstrated through allegiance—which, in truth, may be the best way to describe what it means to truly put your faith in Jesus.

When the New Testament writers talk about faith, they use the Greek word *pistis*. The New Testament contains lots of places where faith has to do with believing that something is true or real, but *pistis* means more than intellectual assent. Faith is more than simply saying, "I have faith that God exists" or "I have faith that Jesus died and rose again." Theology professor Matthew W. Bates argues that the best word to capture the full scope of what it means to put your faith in Jesus is *allegiance*. He explains that *pistis* "includes ideas that aren't usually associated in our contemporary culture with belief or faith, such as reliability, confidence, assurance, fidelity, faithfulness, commitment, and pledged loyalty."[26]

Fidelity to Jesus.

Commitment to Jesus.

Pledged loyalty to Jesus.

Saying yes to Jesus means giving your allegiance to him. This kind of demonstrative commitment goes beyond intellectual assent that he is our Savior; it embodies a way of life that declares, "Jesus is King!"

When Jesus calls you to repent, he is offering you an opportunity to switch allegiances and follow him as his disciple. He is inviting you to see the world through his eyes, to follow him into a new way of living, to leave behind one kind of kingdom to live in another. Repentance is Jesus' call to rethink your entire view of reality and reprioritize your values. Or, in other words, to live the opposite of how you've been living, of what has been comfortable and natural and easy.

Jesus' invitation to a few fishermen on the shore of the Sea of Galilee was straightforward: "Come, follow me."[27] But though the invitation was straightforward, the implications were incredible: He was asking them to travel from one reality to another not just with their bodies but with their hearts, souls, and minds.

What did these fishermen do? They let go of their most significant attachments to the kingdoms of this world—the nets that fed their families and defined their identities—and chose Jesus.[28] Sure, they still lived in this world, but they fully entered a new reality. Jesus would later say, "They are not of the world [anymore]."[29] They now had to learn how to navigate the worldly kingdoms they found themselves in as citizens who belonged to a heavenly Kingdom.[30]

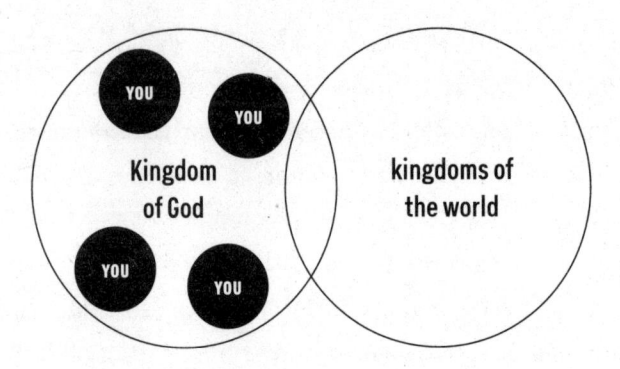

[Diagram: Two overlapping circles. Left circle labeled "Kingdom of God" contains four black dots labeled "YOU". Right circle labeled "kingdoms of the world".]

Two thousand years later, Jesus is still extending this invitation to you and to me: "Come, follow me." This invitation into the Kingdom is an invitation to become his disciples, people who hear from him and do what he says to experience abundant life—to experience shalom. But we have to choose it. We have to repent. We have to give our allegiance to Jesus and follow him so that we can align our kingdoms with the Kingdom of God.

This alignment is going to feel a lot like changing time zones. We're going to have to signal to our bodies, our hearts, and our minds that we've entered a new reality. We'll have to adjust our thinking, our feeling, and our way of being to the patterns of our new Kingdom.

Like Jesus' first disciples, we will have to drop whatever attachments keep us bound to the kingdoms of this world to fully enter this new reality. Dallas Willard says, "Will I listen for God and then obey? For me this tension is what it means to live as one who is learning from Christ how to live in the kingdom of God."[31]

HEAR FROM GOD

Lord, I want to hear from you. Come, Holy Spirit. Speak to me and empower me to do what you say. Amen.

Grab a pen and a notebook or piece of paper. Ask God to bring to your mind anything in your life that pulls you away from the Kingdom of God and back into the kingdoms of this world. Don't overanalyze the things that come to mind; simply write them down. Try to compile a list of eight to ten items.

After you have your list, invite God to draw your attention to the one or two items on your list he wants you to notice. An item that sticks out to you is likely an attachment. Are you willing to drop it to follow Jesus into his Kingdom?

It's that simple, and it's that challenging. *Will I listen? Will I hear what God is saying?* And then . . . *will I obey?*

We'll still feel the pull of the old time zone. Sometimes we might even be tempted to eat when we should be sleeping and sleep when we should be eating. But if we adjust our clocks and stay awake when we feel tired, slowly and steadily we'll find ourselves aligning to our new Kingdom reality.

And entering the Kingdom is the invitation of a lifetime—an invitation to a life of purpose and impact that is beyond our wildest dreams.

CHAPTER 4

CHASING GRANDER DREAMS

Matthew 5:13-16

WHEN YOU WERE A CHILD and someone asked you, "What do you want to be when you grow up?" what did you say? Did it happen?

Maybe you really did become your answer to the question. But my guess is that most of us did not.

I did not become an award-winning recording artist.

I did not become an Olympian or the first female basketball player in the NBA.

I did not become a world-renowned brain surgeon. (I don't even like touching raw chicken, so I'm okay with this outcome.)

Have you ever thought about what your life would have been like if your childhood dreams had come true?

My guess is that many of us had dreams of making our mark on the world in an acknowledged and celebrated way. And even after those unrealistic ambitions faded into reality, I think we all still long to be significant. We want to matter in some way.

Imagine with me again that you are sitting on that hillside overlooking the Sea of Galilee, listening to Jesus teach, and he begins to cast a vision for your life that is grander than anything you ever imagined in your childhood dreams. You and those sitting around you on that hillside are not part of *Forbes*'s "30 under 30," a collection of the brightest young entrepreneurs and rising leaders. Your faces do not grace the pages of *People* magazine's "Beautiful Issue." You aren't even the leaders of *Outreach* magazine's "Fastest-Growing Churches."

You are unknowns.

The poor in spirit.

The meek.

The persecuted.

And Jesus has the audacity to say to you,

> "You are the salt of the *earth*. . . .
> You are the light of the *world*."
> **MATTHEW 5:13-14** (EMPHASIS MINE)

Did you catch that? Not just "You are the salt of your neighborhood." Not just "You are the light of your office building." In this ragtag collection of ordinary people, Jesus sees a community that will impact *the whole world!*

The very idea is absurd—but we need to pause here for a moment of self-reflection. If the idea of impacting the whole world fires us up to go out and conquer, let's be cautious and check our motives. Sometimes we can have a good vision, even a God-ordained vision, but without an awareness of our own inadequacy, we can pursue it with an inflated belief in our own abilities. And when pride begins to overshadow a proper dependence on God, we will charge into the vision with tactics from other kingdoms. The kingdoms of this world are ordered by power, success, and control and are obsessed with winning. When we don't grasp the absurdity of the vision Jesus has for us, our own ambition can eclipse the desire to advance his Kingdom.

And that causes all sorts of problems.

Consider the early days of Apple. In the late 1970s, Apple had grown beyond the point that all the employees knew each other on sight. So they decided, like grown-up companies do, that they should all have name badges. These badges were numbered based on the order in which employees had joined the company.

In his book *Accidental Empires*, Robert Cringely explains the problem with this approach:

> Steve Wozniak was declared employee number 1, Steve Jobs was number 2, and so on.
>   Jobs didn't want to be employee number 2. He didn't want to be second in anything. Jobs argued that he, rather than Woz, should have the sacred number 1 since they were co-founders of the company and J came before W in the alphabet. . . . When that plan was rejected, he argued that the number 0 was still unassigned, and since 0 came before 1, Jobs would be happy to take that number. He got it.[1]

You and I might not lead one of the most successful companies in the history of the world, and we might not be as blatant in our quest for honor and achievement, but don't you still have a gnawing desire to be first?

I feel it. For me, it comes in the form of wanting recognition and opportunities (and feeling underappreciated and underutilized when I don't get them). I'd never say aloud, "I want to be number one!" but I can feel a pang of anger or hurt or frustration when opportunities I want are seized by or given to others. I can fall prey to the lies that the ruler of the kingdoms of this world whispers in my ear: *You are more gifted than that person. It should be you stepping into that opportunity.*

Maybe for you this desire to be number one shows up in your ambition to have the corner office, the nicest house on the block, the most Instagram or TikTok followers of those in your social circle. Perhaps it's about being viewed as the best mom, the best worship leader, the best friend. To you, the deceiver might say, *You deserve this! You've earned this! You really are the bomb!*

We long for significance. That's a good thing! We want our lives to matter. It can be tricky to hold ambition and humility in the same heart, however.

How do the desires for power, success, and control show up in your life? If we're not careful, even in what we do *for* God, we can seek glory for ourselves. We need constant grace to keep from placing ourselves at the center. And that grace can be found in Jesus' words about salt and light.

Salt and Light

Here's what Jesus says to the crowd—and to us:

> "Let me tell you why you are here. You're here to be salt-seasoning that brings out the God-flavors of this earth. If you lose your saltiness, how will people taste godliness? You've lost your usefulness and will end up in the garbage.
>
> "Here's another way to put it: You're here to be light, bringing out the God-colors in the world. God is not a secret to be kept. We're going public with this, as public as a city on a hill. If I make you light-bearers, you don't think I'm going to hide you under a bucket, do you? I'm putting you on a light stand. Now that I've put you there on a hilltop, on a light stand—shine! Keep open house; be generous with your lives. By opening up to others, you'll prompt people to open up with God, this generous Father in heaven."
>
> MATTHEW 5:13-16, MSG

What is salt for? How does light illuminate?
You don't eat salt straight from the shaker.
You don't turn on a light to stare at the bulb.
We salt our food so the flavors already present come to life. We turn on lights to illuminate what is already there, making it visible to human perception.

The Message translation of this passage brings out what I think is the most important truth we need to see: Salt and light aren't meant to be the center of attention. Salt and light are not the focus. As salt, we are to bring out the "God-flavors" of the earth. As light, we are to bring out the "God-colors" of the world.

Our role as salt and light is to reveal the presence of God and the availability of his Kingdom, which means we impact the world not by becoming something great but by making Jesus greatly known.

And notice a couple of truths about what Jesus is saying here:

1. *The pronouncement is communal.* We can't see this in English, but the Greek word rendered *you* in these verses (*humeis*) is plural. In our individualistic culture, we often feel pressure to make something of ourselves, to make an impact on our own. But the Kingdom of God isn't composed of striving individuals. Jesus has a vision for who we will be together as a community of Kingdom-minded people. Together we are the salt of the earth. Together we are the light of the world.

2. *The pronouncement is preemptive.* Jesus says, "You are . . ."—not "You ought to be . . ." or "You could be . . ." or "You should be . . ." *You are.* Jesus makes this audacious pronouncement to people who haven't accomplished anything for the Kingdom yet!

    In the absurd, upside-down, opposite way of the Kingdom of God, your worth isn't based on your accomplishments. You aren't valued for what you've achieved; rather, Jesus has a high view of you *before* you do a single thing for him.

You take a huge step forward in living in the Kingdom of God when you come to grasp that what God really wants from you . . . is you. He wants your heart. He wants your devotion. He wants your allegiance. Many of us spend a lot of our time and energy trying to prove our worth when we are already perfectly and wholly loved.

What if the key to living a purposeful life is simply living into the authentic version of who God made you to be? What if the way to live a truly significant life is by embracing an ordinary life? What if the pursuit of a grander dream is found not in striving but in abiding in Christ?[2] Author Skye Jethani writes,

> Forget the Caesars, and Herods, and Platos. The world doesn't need more YouTube stars or social media celebrities. . . .
>
> . . . The world does not need more ambitious Christians. Rather, salt and light are the outcomes of ordinary lives lived in rich communion with God. Our world desperately needs more of those.[3]

Our world is in desperate need of people who willingly decenter themselves to center Jesus. In the words of John the Baptist: "He must become greater; I must become less."[4]

This group of ordinary men and women sitting on a hillside had an incredible opportunity before them. Jesus was opening an avenue to impact the world that was beyond their wildest childhood dreams.

But there is also a warning in his pronouncement.

"If the salt loses its saltiness, how can it be made salty again? It is no longer good for anything, except to be thrown out and trampled underfoot."

MATTHEW 5:13

Salt that loses its saltiness doesn't have a purpose. Which means we, too, can diminish our influence.

Diminishing Our Influence

Let me tell you about a time when my salt wasn't very salty.

It was 2020, and we were in the throes of the COVID-19 pandemic. Where I live in Illinois, most of our businesses and restaurants were closed a lot longer than in other parts of the country. One particular evening, I decided to order Chili's to-go for dinner. I can't say that Chili's is one of my favorite restaurants, but at the time, they were one of the few restaurants with curbside pickup—and I am a sucker for getting food without having to get out of my car.

I arrived at Chili's at the time the confirmation email said my food would be ready . . . and I waited. And waited. After twenty minutes, my impatience finally got the best of me. I put on the required face mask and went into the restaurant in search of my food. There in the to-go area, I found several other customers waiting. I asked one of the servers about my food, and she told me, "We're working on it."

So I kept waiting. And waiting. I started to grumble to the other customers. Sure, we knew there were staffing shortages, but this was ridiculous. I had a confirmation email with a promised pickup time!

Most of the people in the waiting area were remarkably calm. Everything about my body language communicated that I was not. Finally, after fifty minutes of waiting, my food arrived. I grabbed the bag, didn't say anything to anyone, and left the restaurant in a bit of a huff.

That's when I remembered what was on the face mask I was wearing: the words *Community Christian Church*. And I felt the Spirit's conviction.

It's not like I threw a tantrum in the restaurant, but in a situation when I had the opportunity to be a person of grace, I chose to be a person of self. I tried to imagine what it would be like to walk back into that waiting area—after my visible display of irritation—and ask, "Could I tell you about the difference Jesus has made in my life?" If I were the woman who worked there (or the super chill Uber Eats driver who didn't seem to mind waiting), I would not have been interested in what the church lady had to say.

I didn't bring out any "God-flavors" in Chili's that evening. I didn't give any evidence that "God-colors" were present. Instead, simply because my barbecue ribs were late, I diminished my influence. I tossed flavorless salt into the world.

Here's where we need to be honest with ourselves: As Christians in America, we often don't do a great job of bringing out "God-flavors" and "God-colors" in the world. Many times, we're more interested in winning arguments and imposing our beliefs and preferences on others than in making Jesus known.

Take that face mask I wore, for example. During the height

of the COVID-19 pandemic, many of us let a little piece of cloth become a hill we decided to die on. Some Christians refused to honor the wishes of shopkeepers and restaurant owners who requested that people wear masks. Other Christians began to judge the character of those who weren't wearing the little pieces of cloth. Christians left churches and relationships they had invested in for decades over protocols (or the absence of protocols) involving face coverings.

We let a piece of cloth become a bitterly divisive issue. Some might say, "It wasn't about the mask; it was about what the mask stood for," but I'm not buying it. We gave the masks those meanings. We didn't have to. We could have just seen them as, well, masks.

Instead, what did people see when we dug in our heels over our opinions? Our self-centeredness. And when that was pointed out, rather than opening ourselves humbly to correction, we doubled down and fought harder.

Take any hot-button cultural issue, and you'll find Christians treating the opposition—even other Christians—poorly. We've lost the respect of many outside the church who are watching.

We've diminished our influence. Our salt has lost its flavor.

Sometimes the people we want to blame for our diminished influence are the very people we are supposed to be reaching with the Good News of Jesus. When those outside the church have criticized us, we've mistaken their criticism for persecution. When we don't get our way in social, cultural, or political endeavors, we mistake our diminished influence and loss of power for oppression. Sometimes this perceived "persecution" is even used to justify our own bad behavior or to rally the troops to regain control. This isn't being salt and light. It's just becoming another party sowing division.

Diminished influence is not the same thing as persecution. And a lot of the time, diminished influence is less about the people around us and more about how we're stewarding the Kingdom calling we've been given.

Rather than blaming people in the world when we don't like the way our society is going, what would it look like if we started with self-reflection? If we asked ourselves, *How have we contributed to where things are now? How have our actions and reactions led us further from where we want to be? How have we contributed to our diminished cultural influence?*

HEAR FROM GOD

Lord, I want to hear from you. Come, Holy Spirit. Speak to me and empower me to do what you say. Amen.

Ask God to bring to your mind instances when your words, attitude, or behaviors may have diminished your influence. What did you do or say? Why did you do or say it?

What were the "God-colors" and "God-flavors" that you could have brought out in that situation?

Your worth isn't based on your accomplishments. You are already perfectly loved. Spend some time thanking God that his grace covers all your mistakes. Ask him for new opportunities to live out your role as salt and light. Commit yourself to being led by his Spirit in those opportunities.

In some places we may have lost the opportunity to reveal the presence of God and the availability of his Kingdom. The "God-flavors" and "God-colors" can still be found in those places, but we may not get to play a role in bringing them out.

Wouldn't it have been better to lose some arguments?

Wouldn't it have been better to not get our way in some situations?

After all, the Kingdom of God is never at stake. It cannot be shaken. Jesus remains on his throne. He doesn't need us to fight the wrong battles.

Still, in his grace, I do believe God will give us other opportunities to season and shine. To take hold of those opportunities, however, we need to learn to live into our calling as salt and light.

The Opposite

Years ago when I lived in the city of Chicago, a small Bible-study group I was part of decided we wanted to serve together in some way. We offered ourselves to a nearby refugee resettlement agency, and they asked us to take a refugee family under our wing. We were assigned a young couple who had just arrived from Myanmar. I can't imagine what it would be like to flee your country, the only home you've ever known, and find yourself plopped down in the middle of downtown Chicago. Our appointed couple was friendly but also a bit shy. He spoke some broken English; she spoke none. But a few months after their arrival, they communicated to us that she was pregnant with their first child.

Well, whether they realized it or not, their baby now had about ten American aunties and uncles. My group put out a call, and we had so much fun collecting clothes, toys, and all the other necessities for raising a baby. I even risked looking like a complete fool dragging an empty stroller I'd bought off Craigslist onto the "L" train!

And then we threw a baby shower. Everyone came together in my apartment, and we were excited to shower our new friends with gifts. It was all fun—until the man broke down in tears. That's when I realized this might all be a bit overwhelming for them. We halted the gift giving and decided to just eat cake and play a game or two. We figured we could just bag up the gifts and send them home with the couple later.

When the evening came to an end, I asked if we could all circle up for a moment to pray for this new baby's arrival. The couple agreed, and we stood in a circle, but then the man started crying again. I wasn't sure what to do, but he asked if he could say something to the group.

He told us his tears were tears of joy. "You must understand," he said, "I didn't have pants until I was five years old. I didn't have shoes until I was a teenager. And now I am here, and my baby has all these things before she is even born. I am thanking God for that."

And with that, a dozen people were crying.

Contrast this moment with our instincts. If our group had reacted out of those, we might have gotten mired in debates about immigration policy and refugee quotas. We could have become overwhelmed with concerns about the impact immigration has on our cities, our employment opportunities, and our families. We might have chosen to hoard our salt and dim our lights out of an impulse for self-protection. And we would have missed out on forming a beautiful relationship with precious human beings who experienced God's love in a powerful, tangible way. We would have forfeited the opportunity to join God in bringing more of his Kingdom to earth.

I'm not saying that policy debates about immigration aren't complicated and consequential. But here's what I am saying: We often miss what God wants to do when we, as ordinary followers of Jesus, listen to the fear-driven shouts of our self-preservation instincts and scarcity mentality. The Kingdom won't show up in our everyday lives until we choose the opposite.

Remember—salt and light aren't meant to be the center of attention. Salt and light are not the focus. And they certainly are not supposed to be hoarded. Bringing out the "God-flavors" and "God-colors" in the world means living in a way that's the opposite of our human instincts: to willingly decenter ourselves and instead center Jesus.

What does this mean in practical terms? How do we live this out?

I think it means that rather than asking,

What do I think?
What do I want?
How is this impacting me?
How do I get my way?

we ask,

How can I help reveal Jesus and the upside-down way of his Kingdom in this moment?

We proactively look for ways to reveal the love and grace of Jesus in conversations and situations we find ourselves in. We stop centering ourselves in our lives, and instead seek first the Kingdom.[5]

We welcome and bless the strangers among us.[6]

We include the lonely coworker in our office gatherings.

We patiently listen to the person we don't agree with.

We forgive the family member who insensitively mocked us.

We offer dignity and respect to people whose lifestyles unnerve us.

We consider the needs of our neighbors when we exercise our right to vote.

We step into the grander dream Jesus has for us to spend our lives spreading "God-flavors" and "God-colors" in the world.

Salt and light can't happen when we spend all our energy staying where we're comfortable, when we center ourselves, dig in our heels, and fight to get our way. We become salt and light when we have the courage to deny ourselves, take up our cross, and follow Jesus.[7]

What would our world look like today if we, as the Kingdom community of Jesus, stopped looking to win the arguments, to impose our beliefs and preferences on each situation, and instead aimed to sprinkle the salt of grace and shine the light of love into all the hard places?

What would be different if we no longer participated in all the bickering and turmoil we've experienced and instead faced every challenging issue and situation with the question *How can we help reveal Jesus and the upside-down way of his Kingdom in this moment?*

What if we determined to move forward as salt and light? What might happen?

I suspect what would happen is what Jesus intended for salt and light to do: that the world around us would start to say, "Whoa, something tastes different here. Something looks different here."

And they would "taste and see that the LORD is good."[8]

For as we live as the salt of the earth, as we shine as the light of the world, Jesus is the One the people around us see. Jesus is the One they begin to know. He is the One who is lifted up. And when that happens, the world begins to change.

Yes, like that ragtag group of people sitting on a Galilean hillside, most of our names will end up lost to history. But in the end, we will discover that our childhood dreams were way too small.

We were made not to win accolades, titles, and trophies. We were made to "reign with [Christ]"[9] in "a kingdom that cannot be shaken."[10]

So let's put childish things behind us. Let's begin to live for a grander dream.

CHAPTER 5

LIVING THE SCRIPTURES

⟶ Matthew 5:17-20 ⟵

A FEW YEARS AGO, I learned that there are two kinds of people in the world:

1. those who love *Pride and Prejudice*
2. those who despise any mention of Mr. Darcy

If you're like me, someone who loves the classic Jane Austen novel chronicling the unlikely love story between the feisty Miss Elizabeth Bennet and the enigmatic Mr. Darcy, you might be surprised by this. But when I referenced the work in a social media post, I was taken aback by the passionate responses it evoked. Some people—mostly women but a few brave men—professed their undying love for Jane Austen's characters. Others—mostly men but a few fierce women—expressed that even the mention of Mr. Darcy's name made their stomachs turn. And apparently they are not alone in their disgust. Mark Twain himself wrote, "Every time I read that mangy book, 'Pride & Prejudice,' I want to dig [Austen] up & beat her over the skull with her own shin-bone!"[1] Yikes.

Some books we're probably going to fight about until the end of time.

Including, no doubt, the Bible.

The Bible has been a source of profound influence and inspiration throughout history as well as a spark for fierce debates and controversy. Disagreements over biblical interpretation have led to schisms as large as the Protestant Reformation and as personal as family estrangements. People have argued over whether the Bible is a history book or a rule book or a guidebook, whether it is trustworthy and true or unreliable and false. Every generation has its own set of doctrinal disagreements that seem to dominate discussions about the Bible. I imagine we'll argue about this book until Jesus returns.

But what if, in the Kingdom, *how* we wrestle with this book matters just as much as the convictions we draw from it?

Jesus and the Pharisees

Almost from the moment Jesus started his public ministry, he butted heads with a group of people, the Pharisees, over the Bible that existed at that point in time: a collection of books that they called the Law and the Prophets (what Christians today call the Old Testament). There's quite a bit of irony in this, don't you think? After all, Jesus is the Word of God.[2] He is the God who inspired the Scriptures. For a group of people to argue with him over interpreting those Scriptures would be like a visitor in an art gallery arguing with the artist about the true meaning of her paintings.

Of course, the Pharisees didn't recognize that they were arguing with God. Yet even in his humanity, Jesus demonstrated the high value he places on Scripture. The Gospels show us that Jesus deeply knew and regularly quoted the Law and the Prophets. He held Scripture in high esteem. He relied on it in his own spiritual battles.[3] He constantly drew from it in his conversations and his teaching.[4] He viewed it as authoritative.[5]

And yet many in the religious community accused Jesus of dishonoring and disregarding the Scriptures. The Pharisees knew the Scriptures like the backs of their hands, and they believed they were the ones upholding the law. And because Jesus was speaking of and applying the Scriptures in ways that didn't always line up with what they believed, they charged Jesus with casting the Scriptures aside. From their perspective, Jesus was breaking the law.

But before we just dismiss the Pharisees as the bad guys in the gospel story, let's make sure we are considering them rightly. After all, in the middle of conflicts about the Bible, it's easy to forget the fundamental truths that exist outside the disagreements. The Pharisees still carried inherent dignity as people made in the image of God, as do the people on the other side of our arguments. Yes, the Pharisees were fallible people, but so are we, and so are the people we find ourselves in conflict with.

The Pharisees often get a bad rap. Let's not forget, the main reason they butted heads with Jesus was not because they were insincere in their beliefs but because they were passionate about them. They thought the cause they were fighting for was noble. I wonder if the stories about the Pharisees are given to us not so we can stand in judgment of them but so we can learn from them. If we're willing to recognize the pharisaical tendencies in ourselves, we might avoid the pitfalls that ensnared these committed religious people.

You may have heard that the Pharisees added a bunch of rules to the law, and that's true—but in doing so, they had at least partially good intentions. The Pharisees wanted to make the law more practical and doable for ordinary people. For example, take the law about adultery. In the book of Leviticus, we read, "If a man commits adultery with another man's wife—with the wife of his neighbor—both the adulterer and the adulteress are to be put to death."[6] The Pharisees took this command and added to it. They said things like "How about we don't execute adulterers? Let's just fine them a sum of money instead."

Their willingness to make the law more doable caused a rival, stricter sect of Judaism known as the Essenes to derisively refer to the Pharisees as "seekers of smooth things"[7]— wanting to smooth out the law and make it easier to follow. New Testament scholar Scot McKnight suggests that in this way, the Pharisees might have been viewed as the first-century progressives.[8]

Another way the Pharisees tried to make the law more doable was by adding rules to clarify it. Because the Pharisees wanted people to follow Scripture, they created layers of boundaries and expectations to ensure people would get things right.

For example, take the law about the Sabbath.[9] The people of Israel were to honor the Sabbath, but what did that mean? The Pharisees tried to clarify it by saying things like "Here are thirty-nine rules to follow so that you don't end up working on the Sabbath." They saw their traditions—their rigorous alignment with the Scriptures—as the true way to follow God, and they believed that those outside their tradition were not as pleasing to God. In this way, McKnight goes on to suggest, the Pharisees could have also been considered the first-century conservatives.

The reality is that the Pharisees were popular with the people. Their teachings appealed to ordinary Jews in the first century. Pastor Rodney Reeves writes,

> We use the term *Pharisee* as a synonym for hypocrite. But no one in Jesus's day thought that way. To the Jewish people the Pharisees were more devoted to God's word than anyone else. They were the lay leaders of Israel, dedicated to study the Scriptures (without pay!) and to teach the people what it takes to maintain covenant obedience.[10]

But then Jesus arrived on the scene, and the Pharisees now had a problem. This rabbi in Galilee seemed to think that he, too, could interpret the law for the people. He was preaching a new understanding of the Kingdom of God. He was doing miracles. He was speaking with authority and drawing huge crowds. To the Pharisees, Jesus had become a threat.

They accused Jesus of breaking the law because he wasn't

following their interpretation of the law. One of the thirty-nine clarifying rules the Pharisees had made about the Sabbath was that no one was allowed to take something "from one domain to another,"[11] but Jesus told a paralyzed man to carry his mat on the Sabbath![12] Another Sabbath rule prohibited "reaping,"[13] but Jesus didn't intervene when his disciples picked heads of grain and ate them![14] The Pharisees believed that Jesus was lowering the bar on faithfulness to God's commands.

But once again Jesus was going to upend expectations. He was going to challenge his listeners on that hillside in Galilee by provoking them to rethink what it meant to live out the Scriptures. In his Kingdom, *how* we live the Bible matters just as much as the convictions we hold from it.

Jesus' View of Scripture

The religious leaders may have appeared pious, but Jesus' next stop in the Sermon on the Mount was about to show how much they were missing the mark. Matthew 5:17-20 has been called "the most significant passage in the entire Bible on how to read the Bible"[15] because in it (combined with the section that follows) Jesus reveals a deeper way to read Scripture than we might be used to. His way is the opposite of the way many committed religious people tend to use the Bible.

First, Jesus counters everything the Pharisees believe about his view of Scripture:

> "Do not think that I have come to abolish the Law or the Prophets; I have not come to abolish them but to

fulfill them. For truly I tell you, until heaven and earth disappear, not the smallest letter, not the least stroke of a pen, will by any means disappear from the Law until everything is accomplished. Therefore anyone who sets aside one of the least of these commands and teaches others accordingly will be called least in the kingdom of heaven, but whoever practices and teaches these commands will be called great in the kingdom of heaven."

MATTHEW 5:17-19

Life in the Kingdom of God, Jesus says, includes practicing and teaching the commands of Scripture. Jesus' expectation is that his disciples will treasure Scripture the way he treasures it. He says that those who follow the teachings of the Law will be called great in the Kingdom, while those who disregard these teachings (and teach others to disregard them) will be called least in the Kingdom. Jesus makes it clear that he hasn't come to throw out the Law.

Nothing too surprising yet. The ordinary people listening to Jesus would assume that Scripture matters, just as committed followers of Jesus do today. But what Jesus says next will make everyone's head spin.

"I tell you that unless your righteousness surpasses that of the Pharisees and the teachers of the law, you will certainly not enter the kingdom of heaven."

MATTHEW 5:20

Jesus was not lowering the bar on faithfulness to Scripture; he was raising it! He was calling his disciples to a deeper way of reading and living out the Scriptures, and he said that in this way his followers must surpass the righteousness of the Pharisees and the teachers of the law. This would shock Jesus' listeners! After all, the Pharisees and teachers of the law were considered the most righteous people around. They were meticulous about following the law. And yet, according to Jesus, they had it all wrong—and this all revolves around righteousness.

Righteousness is one of those words that can be hard to understand. Sometimes it stirs up negative feelings. When we hear it, we might think of people who seem self-righteous, looking down their noses at others. If we hear someone say they aspire to be righteous, we might consider them arrogant. And yet righteousness is at the heart of what Jesus calls us to in his Sermon.

Sometimes pastors explain righteousness with a play on words. They'll say, "Righteousness means we are in a *right relationship* with God because of what Jesus accomplished for us through his death and resurrection." They'll quote Paul, who says, "Therefore, since we have been declared righteous by faith, we have peace with God through our Lord Jesus Christ."[16] They'll explain that righteousness is something bestowed on us through faith in Jesus. They might say something like "We can't do anything to earn righteousness; it is a gift from God that we receive through faith."

None of that is incorrect, of course. But when Jesus talked of righteousness in the Sermon on the Mount, his death and resurrection were still a future reality. If we read Paul's use of the word *righteousness* back into Jesus' teaching in the Sermon, we miss what he wanted his listeners there on the hillside to understand.

For a first-century Jew, righteousness involved maintaining fidelity to the covenant relationship God had established with Abraham—that is, obeying the law God had given to Moses. When Jesus spoke of righteousness, this group of Jewish men and women gathered on a hillside in Galilee would have understood that he was talking about their behavior. In the Sermon, *righteousness* refers to "behavior that conforms to the will of God as taught by Jesus."[17] But the behavior Jesus was talking about wasn't just external; it was "whole-person behavior that accords with God's nature, will, and coming kingdom."[18] When Jesus talked about righteousness here, he was talking about something beyond doctrinal correctness or behavior modification. He was talking about a way of living that is good from the inside out. He was talking about a Kingdom way of life.

So when Jesus called his disciples to a righteousness that "surpasses that of the Pharisees," he was saying that the way the Pharisees were living out the Scriptures was not leading to this Kingdom way of life. Rodney Reeves explains,

> Throughout the entire Sermon on the Mount, Jesus is claiming that the Pharisees are not reading the Scriptures rightly. If they did, then their lives would look like the kingdom of heaven on earth.[19]

How we live the Bible matters. If the way we are reading, interpreting, and applying Scripture isn't bringing more of the Kingdom of God to earth, we're not handling Scripture correctly.

The Pharisees followed the law, but they forgot the heart of the law, teaching a form of righteousness that was lifeless and incomplete. They missed the most important thing that undergirds all God's commands: love.

Now, before we pile our disgust on these religious leaders, it would serve us well to take an honest look in the mirror. Are there ways that we do this too? How might our approach to interpreting and applying Scripture be missing the foundation of love?

Let's consider how we handle difficult topics—say, gender and sexuality. When we approach Scriptures that deal with challenging topics like these, it is important to keep three realities in mind:

1. *There aren't multiple valid interpretations of Scripture.* God, working through inspired authors, is communicating specific truth to us. There is a right interpretation of each part of Scripture, an original meaning God intended.

2. *There are many ways we can incorrectly interpret a Scripture passage.* We all approach the text with our own biases and experiences and assumptions. We can easily read into a passage what we want to see there. We also live far removed from the cultures the Bible was written in and written to. What we might consider a clear reading of a passage can be wildly incorrect if we don't understand

the cultural context or the meaning of words when the text was written. As a popular social media meme notes, two thousand years from now, people will not understand the difference between a "butt dial" and a "booty call." Similarly, our English translations of cultural idioms and assumptions can easily cause us to miss what's actually going on. That is what makes interpreting the Bible so challenging!

3. *The only person in history who has correctly interpreted and applied every Scripture is Jesus.* The rest of us are all fallible to misunderstanding. This doesn't mean that we throw our hands up in the air and say, "Truth is unknowable!" But it does mean that even as we develop convictions about how to correctly interpret and apply challenging passages in the Bible, we must hold those convictions alongside a healthy dose of humility and teachability.

Yet our instinct is to claim absolute certainty in each debate and align ourselves with a group of people who interpret Scripture the way we interpret it. One group tends to smooth out what Scripture says to make it more doable for ordinary people. Another tries to clarify what Scripture says with rules that distinguish "right" from "wrong" and expects everyone to follow their clarifications.

Does this sound familiar?

Inevitably what happens is that people in both groups find their way onto social media, where we shout at each other that anyone who doesn't agree with our way of interpreting Scripture is not following God correctly. We convince ourselves that since our interpretation of Scripture is the right interpretation, we are justified in having a negative view of those on the other side. We justify our denouncements. We justify our feelings of superiority. We justify our condemnations. We're poised to cancel each other just like the Pharisees tried to cancel Jesus.

Our lack of love reveals we're completely missing what Jesus is telling us . . . because *how* we live the Bible matters just as much as the convictions we hold from it.

Greater Righteousness

I was about five years old, sitting next to my mom on a metal folding chair in the basement of a Baptist church (or as we church people like to call it, the "fellowship hall"), when a formative reality about love—or the lack of it—took root in my heart. Surrounding us were thirty or forty others who also faithfully attended the Wednesday-night prayer meetings.

Once a month, members would stay after the weekly gathering to conduct official church business, such as voting on whether someone could become a member of the church or whether someone could be baptized. (That one always confused me. I couldn't find any stories in my children's Bible where the disciples asked for a show of hands before agreeing to dunk someone.)

That night's business meeting included an important agenda

item: voting on who would hold positions on the church's various leadership teams for the coming year.

I can still feel the confusion, sadness, and anger that welled up in my five-year-old heart as I watched one gentleman in the church—let's call him Bob—give a passionate speech about why a particular woman in the church—let's name her Jill—did not meet the qualifications for leadership. You see, Jill was divorced, and in those days, divorce was the hot-button topic in Christian circles.

My five-year-old self had overheard whispers that Jill's husband had betrayed her—that she had come home early from work one day to discover him with another woman. Jill moved across the country to start her life over. She became part of our church community, and eventually someone nominated her to serve on a leadership team.

Bob quoted some Scriptures about divorce—I don't remember which ones—in his argument to disqualify her. But the scene remains vivid and fixed in my memory for this reason: Jill was sitting just a few seats away from me, tears welling up in her eyes and rolling down her cheeks as Bob spoke from his open Bible and laid out his argument. She didn't move. She didn't speak. And no one else spoke up for her either.

When the roll call was finished, Jill was voted down, and I can still cry five-year-old tears when I think about it.

My guess is that many people have left churches or even Christianity after similar experiences—both the Jills in the world and the watching five-year-olds. We inflict so much pain on each other.

This is why Jesus calls us to a *greater righteousness*, to a way of living out the Scriptures built on a foundation of love. Later in the book of Matthew, he says,

> "'Love the Lord your God with all your heart and with all your soul and with all your mind.' This is the first and greatest commandment. And the second is like it: 'Love your neighbor as yourself.' *All the Law and the Prophets hang on these two commandments.*"
> MATTHEW 22:37-40 (EMPHASIS MINE)

Everything in the Law and Prophets hangs on loving God and loving people. Jesus is telling us that in his Kingdom, without love, we can't honor the Scriptures. We may be interpreting a particular text correctly, but if how we handle that text doesn't include love for God and love for our neighbor, we are still missing the mark by Jesus' standard.

Jesus isn't after mere doctrinal correctness and external conformity to a list of commands. He's also not asking us to smooth out the teachings of Scripture that make us uncomfortable. The greater righteousness he desires is about *how* we live out the Scriptures.

To walk in the way of Jesus isn't just to believe the right things. It's not even just to do the right things. It's to have the right heart. As author Skye Jethani says, "[Jesus] doesn't merely desire people who appear good, or even those who do good; He wants people who are good."[20]

Jesus wants to give you and me new hearts. This work of transformation happens as he helps us internalize and live out the Scriptures the way he lived them out during his earthly ministry. Through the work of the Spirit, God wants to transform us from the inside out to embody his Kingdom way of love.

The Opposite

A righteousness that surpasses that of the Pharisees is a righteousness that surpasses the "I have the right understanding; they have the wrong one" polarizing attitude that is currently dominating our cultural and church landscape. The righteousness of a Kingdom life is a whole-person way of being in the world that conforms to God's loving nature and will.

Of course, this isn't easy, and we're never going to do it perfectly. I think back to an event I attended where I witnessed God at work in the hearts of many women and men. The time concluded with prayer and commissioning, and I had the privilege of anointing and praying over about a half dozen people who sensed the Spirit of God moving in their lives.

But then the next day I opened social media and saw a critical post from someone who hadn't been at the event. This person questioned the trustworthiness of several participants. He declared that the prayer-and-commissioning time was nothing but a sleep-deprived, smoke-and-mirrors, manipulative sham.

Now, I don't jump into social media arguments. But I can tell you that I began formulating denouncements in my head. I don't know about you, but I can stew on this kind of stuff, contemplating all the things I'd like to say. In this moment, I found myself thinking, *How self-righteous do you have to be to post something like that? Glad I'm not like that.*

And then I put my phone down and opened my Bible to the passage my Lenten devotional pointed me to for that day.

> To some who were confident of their own righteousness and looked down on everyone else, Jesus told this parable: "Two men went up to the temple to pray, one a Pharisee and the other a tax collector. The Pharisee stood by himself and prayed: 'God, I thank you that I am not like other people—robbers, evildoers, adulterers—or even like this tax collector. I fast twice a week and give a tenth of all I get.'
> "But the tax collector stood at a distance. He would not even look up to heaven, but beat his breast and said, 'God, have mercy on me, a sinner.'
> "I tell you that this man, rather than the other, went home justified before God. For all those who exalt themselves will be humbled, and those who humble themselves will be exalted."
>
> **LUKE 18:9-14**

Of course, I could have decided that this passage was for the person I was upset with, but thankfully the Spirit within me prompted me to recognize that these words were for me. My internal condemnation of that person was no different from his external condemnation of the people who attended the conference. Both condemnations were void of love. Through engaging the Scriptures, God gave me the transformative prayer I needed in that moment: *God, have mercy on me, a sinner.*

HEAR FROM GOD

Lord, I want to hear from you. Come, Holy Spirit. Speak to me and empower me to do what you say. Amen.

Ask God to bring to your mind a person or group of people whom you view as inferior or have judged or condemned because they hold different views about Scripture from yours.

What might it look like to love that person or group of people?

Are you willing to love them?

Just to be clear, doing the opposite of the Pharisee does not mean devaluing Scripture. Remember, Jesus warned against setting aside any of its commands. And as Paul writes in his second letter to Timothy, "all Scripture is God-breathed and is useful for teaching, rebuking, correcting and"—notice what Paul says here—"*training in righteousness*, so that the servant of God may be thoroughly equipped for every good work."[21]

The Scriptures are given to us for "training in righteousness," for training in this whole-person way of being in the world that conforms to God's will. When I came across the story of the Pharisee and the tax collector during my morning reading, God used his Word to train me, turning my condemnation of another into conviction and repentance in my own heart. When we engage with the Bible, the Holy Spirit is actively involved in using the words on the page to transform, equip, and empower us for Kingdom living. Scripture is given to us to lead us in the way of righteousness.

Where we often go wrong is in the way we treat people who

disagree with our convictions and interpretations. Sometimes we angrily condemn them, mistreat them, and make pronouncements or private judgments about their lives and eternal destination. Sometimes we label them with ugly terms, assume we know their motivations, and set ourselves up as better and more enlightened than them.

And sure, the people who don't interpret Scripture like we do might be wrong. Let's go ahead and assume they are wrong and we are right. Jesus' words in this passage should cause us to humbly pause regardless. We can hold the theological high ground and still not be acting admirably.

The opposite choice is *not* to let go of your convictions about the teachings of Scripture. Rather, keep studying Scripture. Keep opening your heart to how the Spirit wants to use the words on the page to bring about your own transformation. Remain faithful to the convictions that form out of your engagement with the Bible. You are accountable to God for what you do with his Word.

But the opposite choice *is* to respect and honor the other person's relationship with God. After all, they will answer to him for what they do with his Word just like you will. There is only one Lawgiver and Judge,[22] and thank goodness it isn't me! Thank goodness it isn't you!

Sure, share your convictions about Scripture in respectful, honest ways, but recognize that God hasn't called you to win arguments about the Bible. He can stand behind his Word. He doesn't need you to police it. Let God be God, and let's you and I focus instead on the role he has clearly given us to play in each other's lives: "Love your neighbor as yourself."

Yes, it's hard to do this—because it doesn't come naturally! Later in the Sermon Jesus will say,

> "If you love those who love you, what reward will you get? Are not even the tax collectors doing that? And if you greet only your own people, what are you doing more than others? Do not even pagans do that?"
> MATTHEW 5:46-47

Loving the people who agree with us is not hard. Anyone can do that. But Jesus calls us to a greater righteousness.

CHAPTER 6

LOVING RADICALLY

Matthew 5:21-48

HAVE YOU EVER HAD the perfect comeback? You know, that moment when the just-right retort comes into your mind and out of your mouth and you put someone who has belittled you in their place?

Let's be honest: Rarely do the words come when we need them. I think of another George Costanza moment, a time when he was confident he had the perfect comeback.

George, who works for the New York Yankees, is in a conference room with his colleagues as they discuss the installation of a new scoreboard. A platter of shrimp inexplicably sits on the table, and as the meeting proceeds, George aggressively stuffs his face with shrimp, sharing his opinion through a mouth full of seafood. One of his colleagues leans forward and sarcastically says, "Hey, George, the ocean called. They're running out of shrimp." The whole room erupts into laughter, and George is left frozen and humiliated.

Later, George tells Jerry, "But then I said to him, 'Oh yeah? Well, the Jerk Store called, and they're running out of you!'"

"Really?" Jerry says. "That's great! You said that to him?"

And that's when George replies, "Well, actually, I thought it up on the way over here."

"Oh, that's . . . not quite the same," Jerry observes.[1]

Isn't that what we all experience when we find ourselves in that wish-I-had-a-comeback moment?

But let's say the perfect comeback did come to you when you needed it, not hours later. Which have you regretted more—the untimeliness of a missed comeback, or the fallout of one that came right on time?

"You Have Heard That It Was Said . . ."

Believe it or not, in the Sermon on the Mount Jesus gives us a foolproof approach to those moments when we're longing for the perfect comeback. If we follow his wisdom, we can be regret free after every confrontation.

This wisdom comes in a section of the Sermon connected to the previous one. After Jesus calls his disciples to a greater righteousness, a Kingdom way of living out the Scriptures that's built on a foundation of love, he goes on to illustrate what this Kingdom way looks like by sharing a handful of practical examples.[2] In each example, he says something like "You have heard that it was said to the people long ago . . ." and then quotes an Old Testament command. These commands are likely very familiar to his audience. They've probably heard their religious leaders teach on them dozens of times. But now Jesus gives *his* interpretation. He explains how these commands are to be lived out in his Kingdom way of love.

We shouldn't view these examples simply as rules to follow. They don't address every situation and circumstance in which we'll find ourselves. But taken together, they begin to show us how a Kingdom person thinks and acts in their relationships with others. Dallas Willard says,

> These are illustrations of what a certain kind of person, the kingdom person, will characteristically do in such situations. . . . Though we are not talking about things one must do to "be Christian" or "go to heaven when we die," we are looking at how people live who stand in the flow of God's life now.[3]

The Kingdom way of living out the Scriptures is a way of radical love. And let me tell you up front: This way of life is challenging. You might even call it absurd.

Let's look at three of Jesus' examples.

When You Want Revenge

Jesus says, "You have heard that it was said, 'Eye for eye, and tooth for tooth.'"[4] If we stopped there, a well-timed comeback feels like the right solution. When I'm insulted, I should insult back. After all, it's right there in the Bible! Eye for eye, tooth for tooth, insult for insult.

The command Jesus is quoting is known as the lex talionis, or "law according to kind."[5] Some form of it is found in several places in the Old Testament,[6] seemingly an in-kind penalty for injuring another person.

Imagine what that kind of retribution might look like. When I was sixteen, a couple of my college-age sister's guy friends challenged me to a game of basketball. Now, not to brag, but back in the day, I was pretty good at basketball. As we played, I was easily dominating them. One of the guys decided that the only way to keep me from scoring was to grab both my arms from behind. The problem was that as he did this, he also tripped me, then tried to hold me up by my arms to stop my fall—and that's how I smacked face-first onto the concrete and chipped my front teeth.

Now, the lex talionis would grant me the right to chip his teeth. Maybe I could have grabbed a hammer and ensured we had matching smiles. Of course, I didn't do that. And I'm guessing you think it is good that I didn't. Which helps us understand something important about the lex talionis.

This law wasn't enacted to require barbaric acts of retaliation; its purpose was to curb violence.

If you grew up with siblings, the deeper purpose of this law may make more sense this way. What if your younger brother took a toy that belonged to you—and you retaliated by taking twelve of his toys? Then he struck back by destroying one of your most precious possessions, and you responded by setting his room on fire. What might have started as a minor infraction could easily escalate into an all-out war!

The lex talionis was meant to prevent someone from striking back with a punishment greater than the first offense. In that way, this law makes sense. It's saying, "The punishment should fit the crime."

So eye for eye, tooth for tooth, insult for insult, social media block for social media block, cold shoulder for cold shoulder, grudge for grudge, lawsuit for lawsuit. You get the picture.

But then Jesus steps in and says,

> "You have heard that it was said, 'Eye for eye, and tooth for tooth.' But I tell you, do not resist an evil person."
> MATTHEW 5:38-39

Wait a minute. Do not resist? Don't stand up for yourself? Don't fight back?

With this interpretation, Jesus is not contradicting the Old Testament lex talionis—he is deepening it. He is challenging us to imagine a way of life in which we don't even feel the impulse toward retaliation. Jesus is challenging us to do the opposite: to respond with an upside-down, counterintuitive act of radical grace toward the person who wronged us.

And then he presents four outlandish situations to drive home his point.

Imagine someone slaps you on the cheek and then you stick out the other cheek! Why would anyone do that? Remain vulnerable after injury?

Imagine someone sues you for your shirt and you give them

your coat as well (which, in Jesus' day, would leave you standing naked in the courtroom!). What would possibly make any of us do that?

When a person in authority or a person who oppresses you (for Jesus' listeners, a Roman soldier) demands something of you, such as forcing you to carry his pack one mile, Jesus suggests you should go *two* miles (that is, do more than what is strictly required of you). That's not how we want to react in this scenario, right?

And when someone who has no rightful claim to be asking something of you asks anyway, Jesus says you ought to give freely.

Now, Jesus *is not* talking about situations of abuse in these illustrations. Sometimes these passages have been misused by predators and their allies to silence and shame victims. If you find yourself in an abusive relationship, please reach out to someone you trust and get help.[7] Jesus would not ask you to stay in a situation where you are being harmed.

Nor is Jesus calling us to passively accept societal evils such as racism or human trafficking. As Dallas Willard points out, "the wrongs in question are clearly personal injuries, not institutional or social evils."[8]

What Jesus *is* talking about are those everyday encounters when something hurtful is said or done or when a person in authority is requiring something of us that we shouldn't have to do. He's talking about the times when we are maligned for our beliefs or mistreated by our adversaries. Jesus is saying, "In my Kingdom, I want you to respond to injustice with such gracious generosity that people will be left speechless." Remember, he is teaching us how to live the Scriptures from a foundation of love, to live as Kingdom people. When a Kingdom person experiences a personal affront, they do the opposite and respond with radical grace.

Are you challenged by this? I certainly am. Whether we experience disrespect or harm from the people who live under our roofs, the people we encounter in our daily lives, the strangers we interact with on the internet, or even those who have been put in authority over us (such as governors and presidents), how easy it is to choose the path of revenge and retaliation! How much harder to do the opposite and respond with acts of radical grace.

We typically don't realize that when we get caught up in the fervor of revenge we are ultimately destroying ourselves. We're becoming trapped by unforgiveness and weighed down by our grudges. We find ourselves standing in the rubble of broken relationships and burned bridges. We're destroying our own shalom. We're destroying the shalom in our families, our churches, our communities. It's why the apostle Paul asks, "Why not rather be wronged? Why not rather be cheated?"[9]

A Kingdom person chooses the opposite of revenge, the opposite of coming up with the perfect comeback. Grounded in a foundation of love, a Kingdom person responds with radical grace.

When You Feel Angry

When we've been wronged, retaliation isn't usually our only impulse. In fact, if we're the kind of person who says, "I never feel tempted to retaliate!" it's probably because we internalize our response—in the form of anger.

Anger is a common human impulse, and Jesus has something important to say about it in his Sermon:

> "You have heard that it was said to the people long ago, 'You shall not murder, and anyone who murders will be subject to judgment.' But I tell you that anyone who is angry with a brother or sister will be subject to judgment."
>
> MATTHEW 5:21-22

Jesus deepens a familiar Old Testament command about murder to help us understand that not doing the worst is not the same as doing the best. He challenges us not to just sit back and congratulate ourselves, thinking, *Hey, I didn't murder anyone today; I'm doing pretty good!* After all, not murdering someone is a low bar for what it means to live out Kingdom love. No, Jesus wants us to look more deeply into our hearts at what may be preventing us from loving others: the anger that can so easily stir up within us.

Now, any therapist will tell you that anger is not a bad thing. Anger is usually an indication of a deeper emotion or feeling. Scripture even says, *"In your anger* do not sin."[10] It's not the anger itself; it's what we *do* with that anger that matters.

The worst part about anger is that we never plan on being angry. Instead, anger has this way of sneaking up on us and surprising us with its intensity. And that intensity can spark impulses that we mistakenly believe are out of our control.

For example, think of yourself behind the wheel of a car. Have you ever felt angry on the road, when you're clearly the superior driver and everyone else is getting in the way? I admit, I have—and I know I'm not alone. I came across a study with a shocking statistic: "Nearly 80 percent of [US] drivers expressed significant anger, aggression or road rage behind the wheel at least once in the past year." Nearly 80 percent of us have been angry drivers! Some of you might be thinking *Only 80 percent?* or *Only once this past year?* Of course, there is a big difference between experiencing the emotion of anger and acting on it. But a lot of us *do* act on it. The study found that in that same year, 51 percent of those surveyed admitted to purposefully tailgating other cars, 47 percent yelled at other drivers, and 33 percent made angry gestures.[11]

Our expressions of road rage are generally passing interactions with strangers we'll never see again. What we do with our anger in other areas of life, however, can inflict a lot more long-term relational damage. Some of us have experienced breakdowns in relationships—we have friends we no longer talk to or family members who are estranged—because arguments about racial tensions, Supreme Court decisions, or theological interpretations have become so heated.

When you find yourself at odds with another person, how do you typically respond? Maybe you're someone who tends to explode. Me? I like to stew. I like to coddle and nurture my anger. In my pride, I think, *I'm right, and that person is so wrong!*

And that's exactly why anger is so dangerous. In Jesus' day, angry people said things like "Raca" (a dismissive term of contempt derived from the sound of clearing spit from your throat) or "You fool!" which carried the weight of the most derogatory terms of our day. These insults—and the ones we say aloud and even just inwardly—are more than mere words. They reveal contempt for another human being. They diminish the value of that human being. These insults are such a serious offense to Jesus that he said they would justify the offender coming under harsh divine judgment themselves.

So in his Sermon Jesus calls us to an opposite way of dealing with anger:

> "If you are offering your gift at the altar and there remember that your brother or sister has something against you, leave your gift there in front of the altar. First go and be reconciled to them; then come and offer your gift."
>
> MATTHEW 5:23-24

Not stewing on anger. Not exploding with anger. Instead, radical humility. Jesus is calling us to be the ones who break through the relational tension to seek shalom.

Notice, Jesus doesn't say, "And there remember that you did something against your brother or sister." He says, "And there remember that your brother or sister has something against you." This means you may have done nothing wrong! Culpability doesn't seem to matter to Jesus in this moment. What matters is that a relationship is broken, and Jesus is telling us to do everything in our power to bring about reconciliation.

And again he uses an absurd example to illustrate his point. Jesus was speaking to people in Galilee, which is in the northern region of Israel. When he spoke of "offering your gift at the altar," his audience would have pictured themselves in Jerusalem, in the southern region of the nation, where the Temple was. His instruction to leave one's gift at the altar, go make things right with the other person, and then come back very likely meant returning to Galilee—ninety miles away—to seek reconciliation. Put one hundred and eighty miles on those sandals! How absurd!

But it drove home the point. Jesus was saying, "In my Kingdom, we're going to do things differently. We're not going to hold on to grudges. We're not going to justify our anger. Instead, even if we're not at fault, we're going to do the opposite. In the Kingdom way of love, we're going to respond with radical humility as we seek reconciliation."

Not too long ago, I got in a little dustup with a colleague, someone with whom I sometimes don't see eye to eye. We are both committed to Jesus and to being friends, but on more than one occasion, we've left each other's presence angry. One day when our conversation went sideways, we parted with the issue unresolved. I got in my car, left the church building, and went home, where I planned to remain for the rest of the day.

But then the Spirit brought to my mind the words of Jesus: "You have heard that it was said to the people long ago . . ."

No! I protested. *I don't want to live like a Kingdom person today, Jesus!* But I have walked with Jesus long enough to know that ignoring him never works out well for me. And so I got back in my car, drove back to the church building, found my coworker, and apologized for how I had treated him.

And you know what? I didn't enjoy it. It felt humbling. I still thought he was wrong about the situation.

But do you know what else happened? I didn't stew over it for the rest of the day. I didn't nurture ill feelings toward him for the rest of the week. I was able to let it go and move forward with peace, and my connection with this coworker reflected a little bit more of the Kingdom way of love than it had the day before.

Maybe, just maybe, Jesus knows what is best.

When You Have Power

Another example Jesus gives of how a Kingdom person lives out the Scriptures will surprise us because the implications reach far more broadly than we might expect.

> "It has been said, 'Anyone who divorces his wife must give her a certificate of divorce.' But I tell you that anyone who divorces his wife, except for sexual immorality, makes her the victim of adultery, and anyone who marries a divorced woman commits adultery."
>
> MATTHEW 5:31-32

If the statistics are correct, more than a third of us have experienced divorce.[12] So before we explore what Jesus is saying here, let's remember that "there is now no condemnation for those who are in Christ Jesus."[13] Yes, Jesus calls his disciples to a Kingdom way of life, but he also extends grace when we fall short. If you have experienced a divorce, I'm sorry you had to go through that. Relational brokenness is painful, and it's even more so when that brokenness happens to our most intimate relationships. Let's figure out what Jesus wants us to see in this passage and move forward from here together.

No matter our story, we would all say that the breakdown of marriages—which can happen not just through official divorce but also through harm that happens within marriages—was not part of God's original design for his creation. Ask any person who has been through that, and they will tell you that the experience was not shalom.

What is God's intention for us in this most intimate relationship? One-flesh-ness. God's intention is that the two become one and remain so for life:

> Some Pharisees came to [Jesus] to test him. They asked, "Is it lawful for a man to divorce his wife for any and every reason?"
>
> "Haven't you read," he replied, "that at the beginning the Creator 'made them male and female,' and said, 'For this reason a man will leave his father and mother and be united to his wife, and the two will become one flesh'? So they are no longer two, but one flesh. Therefore what God has joined together, let no one separate."
>
> MATTHEW 19:3-6

As this passage continues, Jesus states that Moses only permitted divorce because of Israel's hardness of heart. Moses gave instructions about a certificate of divorce because, despite God's intended design for marriage, divorces were happening.

The problem was that Moses' instructions about the certificate had become a license in the hands of many men. Some of them believed that a man could divorce his wife for any reason—even for something as small as burning dinner! A Jewish man could use any reason he wanted to get a divorce if he followed Moses' guidance about the certificate.

Of course, in a society where men had the financial, social, and religious power, divorce was brutal for women. Scholar Jonathan Pennington explains, "It would be extremely difficult for a formerly married woman in first-century Judaism to survive economically and socially without being married."[14] Most women would be forced to remarry simply to survive.

The realities of the context Jesus was speaking to should make us pause and consider the deeper relational implications beneath his instructions about divorce. What was Jesus really doing when he said, "Anyone who divorces his wife, except for sexual immorality, makes her the victim of adultery, and anyone who marries a divorced woman commits adultery"? He was putting a spotlight on the harm those with power were inflicting on those without it. Pennington observes,

> He is pushing the male perpetrator of an invalid divorce to realize that he is actually the cause of his former wife's adultery, not her, by virtue of forcing

her into a remarriage situation when she was wrongly divorced.[15]

Jesus was raising the bar for men! He was saying that no longer could they disregard the security and well-being of those in the more vulnerable position. Men were directly responsible for the desperate situation women would find themselves in, and Jesus was saying that this harmful way of practicing divorce needed to stop. (As a side note, I find it somewhat comical that upon hearing Jesus' words, Jesus' disciples didn't say, "Yes, Jesus, you are right. We shouldn't be flippant about divorce" but rather responded, "If this is the situation between a husband and wife, it is better not to marry."[16] It appears fear of commitment has a long history!)

Jesus was demonstrating that he holds a much higher view of the marriage covenant than many in his day did and that he wants his followers to hold that view too. There's a broader application of this example that teaches all of us, regardless of marital status, how to think and act like a Kingdom person, however. I believe that what Jesus was demonstrating in this conversation about divorce was not just a high value on marriage but also radical solidarity with the vulnerable.

In a culture where women were viewed more like property than partners, Jesus spoke out against the men who were mistreating them. Rather than placate the centers of power or go along with the cultural norms in his society, he did the opposite and stood with those without power, without influence. Jesus consistently resisted the privileged ways of the powerful and demonstrated solidarity with the powerless.

HEAR FROM GOD

Lord, I want to hear from you. Come, Holy Spirit. Speak to me and empower me to do what you say. Amen.

Are there ways you have aligned yourself with the powerful rather than the powerless?

Who are those who are marginalized in your community, in your workplace or school, in your church? What are some ways you could demonstrate solidarity with them?

What is God saying to you in this moment? What will you do in response?

The Opposite

Jesus calls us to a Kingdom way of living out the Scriptures that's built on a foundation of love. It's a radical way of relating with those around us that goes against what our human instincts tell us we deserve. This is what this opposite approach to relationships looks like:

- *Radical humility.* Jesus says, "You have heard that it was said to the people long ago, 'You shall not murder, . . .' but I tell you . . .'"[17]—that the Kingdom way of love goes so much further than that. When we look through Jesus' eyes, we will recognize the value of every human being as a person made in the image of God. Jesus will show us a way of life that refuses to let anger thrive or contempt reign, teaching us to respond to volatile situations with *radical humility*.

- *Radical respect.* Jesus says, "You have heard that it was said, 'You shall not commit adultery.' But I tell you . . ."[18]—that the Kingdom way of love refuses to dehumanize other human beings. Jesus modeled a way of life for us that recognizes the dignity of every person. As we continue to follow him, he will empower us to relate to every person we come across with *radical respect.*

- *Radical solidarity.* Jesus says, "It has been said, 'Anyone who divorces his wife must give her a certificate of divorce.' But I tell you . . ."[19]—that in the Kingdom, we're going to stand with the vulnerable and call the powerful to repentance. As we let Jesus continue his work of transformation in us, we will find that in situations where we might have been tempted to cling to power or get combative or defensive we now desire to respond with *radical solidarity.*

- *Radical transparency.* Jesus says, "Again, you have heard that it was said to the people long ago, 'Do not break your oath, but fulfill to the Lord the vows you have made.' But I tell you . . ."[20]—that the Kingdom way of love will make oaths unnecessary. God will help us become people who are so confident in his love that we can love others with truth and integrity. We won't feel any need to manipulate others with our words. Instead, we'll find freedom in conducting ourselves with *radical transparency.*

- *Radical grace.* Jesus says, "You have heard that it was said, 'Eye for eye, and tooth for tooth.' But I tell you . . ."[21]—that in the Kingdom we can trust God to be the One to set things right. When we follow him, his upside-down, unexpected way of *radical grace* will become our way too.

- *Radical acceptance.* Jesus says, "You have heard that it was said, 'Love your neighbor and hate your enemy.' But I tell you . . ."[22]—that there is freedom in the Kingdom way of love. Imagine not being burdened by hatred. Imagine not feeling the need to separate people into the categories of "good" and "bad." Imagine no longer being afraid. Jesus wants to set us free to experience his shalom. He wants to teach us to live with *radical acceptance*.

With these examples, Jesus isn't giving new laws to follow—he is, as Willard says, describing "what a certain kind of person, the kingdom person, will characteristically do in such situations."[23] When we learn to live out the Scriptures the way Jesus lived out the Scriptures, our lives will begin to reflect his Kingdom way of radical love. This countercultural life will often require us to do the opposite of our natural instincts—instincts that, if left unchecked, will only continue to lead to more of the same polarizing, divisive, relationally messed-up stuff we've been experiencing. If we don't choose the opposite, we'll stay stuck in the same patterns and places we keep finding ourselves in.

Family conversations will remain stifled or fall silent, crippled by the fear of triggering reactions.

Friendships will continue to disintegrate as unacknowledged wrongs and unforgiven wounds destroy trust.

The most vulnerable among us will continue to suffer while we look the other way and shrink back from getting involved.

We will continue to live in the shallows of spiritual maturity, leaving one church after another in search of a place where everyone thinks just like us.

We can choose that way.

Or we can choose the opposite way of the Kingdom and follow Jesus, who closes this section of the Sermon with these words:

"Be perfect, therefore, as your heavenly Father is perfect."
MATTHEW 5:48

The Greek word translated "perfect" here is *teleios*, which means "complete," "mature," or "in full development."[24] *Teleios* is not a call to moral perfection—Jesus knows we are not capable of that. Instead, it is a call to set our hearts on loving every person just as God loves every person. The kind of perfect love Jesus calls us to is a love that is *radically humble* and *radically respectful*. It's a love that embodies *radical solidarity* and *radical transparency*. Ultimately, it is a love that is full of *radical grace* and *radical acceptance*.

Jesus is inviting us to embody the very *radical love* that God himself holds and that Jesus has demonstrated. When we find ourselves in challenging relational situations, we can ask Jesus,

What does your radical way of love look like in this situation? We can hear from God and then do what he says.

And somewhere down the road, we'll be surprised when his Kingdom way of love becomes a little more natural to us. We'll realize, *Hey! Jesus rubbed off on me!* And we, and those around us, will begin to experience Jesus' way of relational flourishing, his way of shalom.

We'll discover that this invitation to Kingdom love is an invitation to be beautiful.

To be whole.

To be free.

CHAPTER 7

PERFORMING FOR THE RIGHT AUDIENCE

Matthew 6:1-18

WHEN WAS THE LAST TIME you used the word *locavore*? The term describes a person whose diet consists only or principally of locally grown or produced food. Maybe I just run in circles where we're too attached to french fries, but I don't even remember hearing that *locavore* is a word, much less one that has ever gotten much traction among my friends.

Locavore was the 2007 US Word of the Year from the editors behind the *Oxford English Dictionary*.[1] Since 2004, the Word of the Year has been meant to capture a word that supposedly not only expresses the ethos or mood of a particular year but also has the potential for lasting cultural significance. Some, of course, stand the test of time more than others.

One Oxford word that seems to have hit the proverbial nail

on the head is the 2013 winner, *selfie*. Can you imagine that there was a time when the word *selfie* didn't exist? At one point, you actually needed *another human being* to take your picture for you! But when the iPhone 4 introduced a front-facing camera, self-directed glamour shots took over social media—pictures taken from outstretched arms, trying to capture just the right angle, trying to portray just the right image. After all, why merely enjoy a sunset at the beach when all your followers could now *see you* enjoying a sunset at the beach?

We all want to be seen. But for some people, this desire has turned deadly. Over a fourteen-year period, 379 people died trying to get the perfect selfie.[2] A tourist fell down a staircase to his death while taking a selfie at the Taj Mahal. A man was gored to death while trying to take a selfie with a bull at the annual bull-running festival in Spain. Three teenagers in Utah were killed by a Union Pacific train while posing for a selfie.

Our desire to be seen can have tragic consequences.

But that doesn't change the fact that deep down we all long to be seen.

We want to know that we are worth noticing. We want to know that we matter. But when our desire for affirmation points us in the wrong direction, we can find ourselves in places that aren't good for us. We can start chasing after approval and applause, even from people we don't know. This can happen at work, in our relationships, on social media, and even in our spiritual journeys.

The opposite of being seen isn't being invisible. It's about who we want to see us—and why.

Hungry to Be Seen

Jesus knows our longing for affirmation is a temptation for us. He knows that chasing after the approval of others is a significant barrier to the flourishing life we are made for. That's why he addresses our craving to be noticed in the next section of the Sermon on the Mount:

> "Be careful not to practice your righteousness in front of others to be seen by them. If you do, you will have no reward from your Father in heaven."
>
> MATTHEW 6:1

This warning acts as a sort of thesis statement for what follows in the next seventeen verses. What Jesus is driving at is the motivation behind our actions. Are we doing our acts of righteousness so that other people will see us and subsequently praise us? Remember, *righteousness* refers to behavior that conforms to the will of God. Jesus is talking about the good things we do, the noble deeds, the praiseworthy actions—things like praying, fasting, and charitable giving. He's warning us that we can do these things with a distorted heart:

> "When you give to the needy, do not announce it with trumpets, as the hypocrites do in the synagogues and on the streets, to be honored by others. Truly I tell you, they have received their reward in full."
>
> MATTHEW 6:2

> "When you pray, do not be like the hypocrites, for they love to pray standing in the synagogues and on the street corners to be seen by others. Truly I tell you, they have received their reward in full."
>
> MATTHEW 6:5

> "When you fast, do not look somber as the hypocrites do, for they disfigure their faces to show others they are fasting. Truly I tell you, they have received their reward in full."
>
> MATTHEW 6:16

If Jesus were sitting across from you in your favorite coffee shop or local diner, how might he offer this warning today? Perhaps he'd say something like this:

"When you pay for the car behind you in the Starbucks drive-through, don't post a video about it on social media. You may rack up a lot of likes and comments, but publicizing your act of kindness calls into question your true motivation. Were you just trying to make yourself look good?

"No, when you feel prompted to do something generous for another person, just do it and let it be. Be anonymous if you can. Don't forget, your Father in heaven sees you and loves being in on the secret with you."

"When you engage in spiritual activities with other people, like praying or singing worship songs, make sure your thoughts are centered on your Father in heaven and not on what the other people in the room might be thinking about you. Otherwise, you might find yourself performing for people as if you were on some kind of spiritual reality-TV vocal competition.

"Instead, when you are engaged in these activities, imagine yourself alone with the Father. When your heart and mind are set on him, God will meet you in that place, and you'll experience something far better than the polite applause of people."

"When you set aside a day to honor God by denying yourself food . . . What's that? You don't ever do this? No, sorry, I'm not talking about intermittent fasting for weight loss. No, I don't mean fasting from social media either. Okay, never mind. Let's just go with the first two examples."

Both in ancient Galilee and today, Jesus is challenging his listeners to be ruthlessly honest, to ask ourselves, *What is at the core of my motivations for doing good?*

Even as I was writing this, a memory came to me, and I felt convicted. I was on a trip to Ecuador with a Christian humanitarian-aid organization that aims to positively influence the long-term development of children who live in poverty. I, along with other pastors and church leaders, had been invited on the trip to explore how our churches might partner with this organization. We met the Ecuadorian staff and toured their headquarters, and then they drove us out to a remote village to visit one of their centers and meet some of the children.

When we arrived at the center, my attention immediately fixated on one of the most adorable youngsters in the crowd. This little guy couldn't have been more than a year old. I approached his mother, who graciously handed him to me. My first instinct? I turned to one of my traveling companions and asked him to take a picture.

I think about that moment often. It might not seem like a big deal to you, but I think it exposed something concerning about my heart. Was I there to love that child? Or was I there for a photo op so I could share a praiseworthy image of myself with my friends?

Just imagine if this story had gone this way:

> Then people brought little children to Jesus for him to place his hands on them and pray for them. But the disciples rebuked them.
>
> Jesus said, "Let the little children come to me, and do not hinder them . . . *for three of you will include this moment in your written accounts of my life, and a story about me blessing kids will be heartwarming and make me look humble and kind.*"
>
> **MATTHEW 19:13-14 WITH A TERRIBLE ADDITION**

Every time I look at that picture with that precious Ecuadorian child, I am reminded of my heart's proclivity to do noble things from questionable motives.

In fact, it's important to note that when Jesus tells us "Do not be like the hypocrites," he is not defining a hypocrite as someone who claims to live a moral life while doing immoral things—he is saying that a hypocrite is someone who does moral things with problematic motives. We tend to reserve the word *hypocrite* for those who violate the ethical standards they espouse, but Jesus uses the word *hypocrite* to describe a person who does the right things for the wrong reasons.

Now, let me clarify that Jesus isn't condemning public behaviors in general. He's not suggesting that we have to take special care to make sure no one notices what we do. After all, Jesus' disciples must have heard him pray—they recorded some of his prayers! Jesus went to the synagogue and publicly read Scripture. He praised the widow who gave all she had, which meant he had to have actually seen what she gave.

These statements from Jesus in the Sermon don't prohibit public deeds, but they draw attention to what the wrong motive is: *to be seen by others.*

But why, exactly, is that such a problem?

The Real Problem

We are hardwired to desire affirmation, and that's not a bad quality in and of itself. In fact, we see this impulse from the earliest stages of our lives. I think of my nephews when they were little. Whether they were attempting a somersault or jumping off a diving board, their constant plea was "Watch me, Aunt Tammy! Watch me!"

The problem enters when the "Watch me!" of childhood

becomes (as it easily can) an adult's unspoken—but more complicated—"Notice me." *Notice the work I'm doing. Notice the outfit I'm wearing. Notice how competent I am. Notice how spiritual I've become.*

The danger with living for the approval of people is that this approach will inevitably clash with our allegiance to Jesus. The apostle Paul asks:

> Am I now trying to win the approval of human beings, or of God? Or am I trying to please people? If I were still trying to please people, I would not be a servant of Christ.
>
> **GALATIANS 1:10**

If I'm chasing the approval of human beings, I will find myself compromising my allegiance to Jesus. Rather than living my days asking,

- *What would Jesus choose in this decision?*
- *How can I best honor God in this relationship?*
- *What would it look like to choose God's Kingdom at this moment?*

. . . I'll find myself contemplating,

- *How can I make sure people think I'm successful?*
- *How can I avoid making that person angry?*
- *Which of these twenty-eight pictures I took in the bathroom mirror will garner me the most social media attention?*

Living for others' approval will divide my allegiance. I can no longer live with the clarity that "Jesus is King!" Now I serve many kings. At times, my boss is king or my friends are king or my significant other is king or the strangers on social media are king.

And Jesus tells us, "If you do [live your life to be seen by others], you will have no reward from your Father in heaven." Basically, if what we're after is the approval of other people, God will leave us to chase it. He's not interested in competing for our attention. As Dallas Willard puts it, "when we want human approval and esteem, and do what we do for the sake of it, God courteously stands aside because, by our wish, it does not concern him."[3]

If Jesus were sharing these words from the Sermon on the Mount today, he likely wouldn't name synagogues and street corners as the places where we're tempted to get others to notice us. But I suspect he would mention social media.

Listen, I enjoy social media. I'm on several platforms and typically engage with them daily. You may have found this book because of something I posted on social media. But in our modern world, these online gathering places are the primary avenues by which we can fall into the trap of living our lives as Jesus warns us against in his Sermon: "to be seen by others."

If you are active on social media, look at your last half-dozen or so posts and ask yourself, *Why did I post that? What was I hoping would happen when I posted that?* Be honest with yourself about your motivations and reflect on your emotions. Did you find your sense of self rising or falling with the likes and comments?

A simple Google search will reveal the ties between social media use and depression, narcissism, anxiety, and other mental-health concerns—but social media can also be a detriment to discipleship. In the face of an ever-present temptation to live from a posture of *Notice me!*, our timelines and newsfeeds draw our attention away from the One who says, "Follow me."

I'm not saying that it is wrong to feel good when people engage with a post! But we need to consistently check ourselves and remain on guard against how these platforms provide an ever-accessible means for us to live our lives for the approval of others.

Part of growing in the Kingdom way of Jesus is recognizing that this need to be noticed can never be truly satisfied by other people. We will never find shalom in social media likes or YouTube views. We are made to be noticed by God.

Wherever you are, pause for just a second. Take a deep breath. Ponder the reality that God sees you. The psalmist writes:

> From heaven the LORD looks down
>   and sees all mankind;
> from his dwelling place he watches
>   all who live on earth.
>
> PSALM 33:13-14

God notices you. And just in case that thought starts to stir up anxiety or fear, let me remind you that he is a loving Father. He created you. He loves you. You are his beloved child. He wants good things for you. He wants you to experience a sense of well-being in the deepest part of your soul. You are already seen by the One who matters most.

HEAR FROM GOD

Lord, I want to hear from you. Come, Holy Spirit. Speak to me and empower me to do what you say. Amen.

Take a moment and breathe deeply. Release any stress in your face, neck, and shoulders. Still your heart before God.

The psalmist reflects:

> You have searched me, LORD,
>   and you know me.
> You know when I sit and when I rise;
>   you perceive my thoughts from afar.
> You discern my going out and my lying down;
>   you are familiar with all my ways.
> Before a word is on my tongue
>   you, LORD, know it completely.
> You hem me in behind and before,
>   and you lay your hand upon me.
>
> PSALM 139:1-5

God notices you. He is present with you in this moment. Ask him to remind you of his love for you.

We are made to be noticed by God. We are designed to find our identity in him. Therefore, as followers of Jesus, we have to discern what may be tempting us to chase the approval and affirmation of human beings instead. The opposite kind of life looks like living for an audience of One.

The Opposite

I live before the Audience of One. Before others I have nothing to prove, nothing to gain, nothing to lose.[4]
OS GUINNESS

When we live in the Kingdom of God, we orient our whole lives around what is honoring and pleasing to God. And yes—doing the opposite of our natural impulse to seek human affirmation will likely require that we risk upsetting or displeasing other people. Most certainly, at times doing the opposite will leave us feeling overlooked, underappreciated, or even ignored. But as Dallas Willard says, "whatever our position in life, if our lives and works are to be of the kingdom of God, we must not have human approval as a primary or even major aim. We must lovingly allow people to think whatever they will."[5]

God sees. God notices. John Calvin observed that "the theatre of God is in the hidden corners."[6] The more we learn to live our lives for an audience of One, the more we will experience freedom from the roller coaster of emotions that accompanies living for the approval and affirmation of human beings. The roots of our identity will grow deep in a foundation much more solid than social media likes.

How do we do this? If we are hardwired to desire affirmation, how do we learn to do the opposite—to release our craving for human approval and live for an audience of One?

Well, right in the middle of this section of the Sermon, Jesus gives us a tool that can align our hearts and minds with his Kingdom:

"This, then, is how you should pray:

> "'Our Father in heaven,
> hallowed be your name,
> your kingdom come,
> your will be done,
>   on earth as it is in heaven.
> Give us today our daily bread.
> And forgive us our debts,
>   as we also have forgiven our debtors.
> And lead us not into temptation,
>   but deliver us from the evil one.'"

MATTHEW 6:9-13

The Lord's Prayer—a Kingdom prayer concerned with Kingdom realities—sits at the center of this section and at the center of the Sermon on the Mount. Whether we recite it or use it as a template for our own prayers, this prayer lifts us out of the smallness of our own self-concern and self-obsession to remind us of larger realities. Consider how each piece of this prayer can help us live for an audience of One:

- *"Our Father."* The beginning of this prayer reminds us that God is a perfect parent who wants us, his children, to flourish. He wants us to experience deep intimacy with him and a sense of well-being in the deepest parts of our soul. "Our Father" is an audacious invitation to address God with the same intimacy that Jesus shares with the Father. We are invited to approach God with the familiarity and boldness of a child running into the open arms of their parent.

- *"In heaven."* We tend to think of heaven as some distant place where we will go after we die, but this is not the meaning Jesus (or the biblical writers) had in mind. The word rendered "heaven" in this prayer literally translates to "in the heavens." It means what we would call the sky or the air around us. This is significant: When we pray to our Father in the heavens, we are praying not to a God who is distant but to a Father who is present in the atmosphere all around us. He is near. We live in the presence of a loving Father who is as close to us as the air we breathe. Our audience of One is always with us.

- *"Hallowed be your name."* In the Bible, a name represents a person's whole being. What does this petition that God be hallowed mean? The word *hallow* means "[to] treat as holy."[7] This part of the prayer expresses a desire to see God truly honored as God—to see him lifted up and glorified. Even though we experience intimacy with God as our loving Father, these words help us remember that he is still to be revered. He is set apart. No one else is like him. He is the audience who matters.

- *"Your kingdom come, your will be done, on earth as it is in heaven."* This is the now-and-not-yet prayer of a follower of Jesus. Jesus has brought the Kingdom near, which means that the Kingdom is available for us to live in now. But the Kingdom is not yet completely here.

Until Jesus returns, he instructs us to pray for more of the Kingdom, more of God's will, to be done on earth as it is in heaven.

This line in the Lord's Prayer has become a centerpiece of my prayer life. I often write it in my journal. It reminds me that the purpose of my life is not to build my own kingdom or even the kingdom of the church I serve. As I pray these words to my audience of One, I reaffirm my allegiance to Jesus as King and my commitment to live in his Kingdom.

- *"Give us today our daily bread."* Scholar N. T. Wright suggests that this line in the prayer "means 'give us, *here and now*, the bread of life which is promised for the great Tomorrow'. Give us, in other words, the blessings of the coming Kingdom—right now."[8] Sure, as we bring our requests to God, we can ask for things like safe travels and good grades. But Jesus is also inviting us to pray big. Pray for the goodness of the Kingdom to come now! Pray for the healing of the Kingdom to come now! Pray for the peace of the Kingdom to come now! When we pray big prayers, we are reminded that we need a big God. Our hope cannot be found in people. It can only be found in our audience of One.

- *"And forgive us our debts, as we also have forgiven our debtors."* The Kingdom way refuses to take an eye for an eye or a tooth for a tooth. Instead, people of the Kingdom extend radical grace. And the prayer reminds us that just as we are called to do this for others, our

Father in heaven will do this for us. We don't have to hide from him. We don't need to be afraid. We can "approach God's throne of grace with confidence, so that we may receive mercy and find grace to help us in our time of need."[9] Why chase after the affirmation of human beings when the shalom we need is available in the presence of our audience of One?

- *"And lead us not into temptation, but deliver us from the evil one."* The final line in this prayer reminds us that we live on a battleground. Peter warned us, "Your enemy the devil prowls around like a roaring lion looking for someone to devour."[10] Every day, the evil one wants to pull us into the kingdoms of this world. Every day we will experience temptations to follow him. But as we pray this prayer, we fix our eyes on our audience of One and remember that he is King. Wright notes,

  > To pray "deliver us from evil," or "from the evil one," is to inhale the victory of the cross, and thereby to hold the line for another moment, another hour, another day, against the forces of destruction within ourselves and the world.[11]

The Lord's Prayer is a Kingdom prayer concerned with Kingdom realities. And I wonder if Jesus gives it to us in the middle of his discourse about seeking the notice and approval of others because he knows that the opposite way requires us to realign our hearts and minds to our audience of One.

The fascinating thing is that as he calls us away from living for the notice and approval of human beings, Jesus doesn't say that our motives should be altruistic. He wants us to be after a reward. Three times in this section of the Sermon, Jesus says,

> "Your Father, who sees what is done in secret, *will reward you.*"
> MATTHEW 6:4, 6, 18 (EMPHASIS MINE)

Jesus promises that when we live our lives before an audience of One, we will be rewarded. And what is the reward? The presence of God. Intimacy with God. Closeness with the King.

Why spend your energy trying to sidle up alongside important people when the almighty God is saying, *Come near*?

Why chase the approval and affirmation of human beings when the Creator of the universe says, *You belong with me*?

Why continue striving for social media likes and the praise of people when your Father in heaven says, *I see you*?

Jesus' invitation here makes me think of C. S. Lewis's lament:

> Indeed, if we consider the unblushing promises of reward and the staggering nature of the rewards promised in the Gospels, it would seem that Our Lord finds our desires not too strong, but too weak. We are half-hearted creatures, fooling about with drink and sex and ambition when infinite joy is offered us, like an ignorant child who wants to go on making mud pies in a slum because he cannot imagine what is meant by the offer of a holiday at the sea. We are far too easily pleased.[12]

So let's put down our phones and stop chasing after everything we think will make us feel valuable or important. Let's stop worrying about how we are perceived or the size of the platform we're influencing.

Let's live for the right audience.

Let's take a deep breath and exhale as we pray, *Our Father in heaven* . . . And then let's listen for his still, small voice whispering in return, *I see you.*

CHAPTER 8

PRIORITIZING THE KINGDOM

Matthew 6:19-34

HOW MUCH MORE MONEY WOULD YOU NEED to feel financially comfortable?

Here's a fascinating revelation: "Studies show that most people, regardless of income, answer the question the same way: We need about 10% more to feel comfortable. Ten percent will make a difference, and whether we earn $30,000 per year or $60,000 or $250,000 or a cool million, just 10% more" feels like it will make an appreciable difference.[1] According to philosophy professor Christopher Kaczor, "when [people] do get that 10%, which typically happens over the course of a few years, they want just another 10%, and so on, ad infinitum."[2]

We all likely have gone through times in our lives when it legitimately feels like we don't have enough money to get by.

I'm not downplaying that by any means. Perspective should cause us to pause just a bit though. "Even the developed world's poor and middle classes are, by global standards, extraordinarily rich. After adjusting for cost-of-living differences, a typical American still earns an income that is 10 times the income received by the typical person in the world."[3] And yet many of us, no matter where we fall on the pay scale, experience stress and anxiety about not having enough.

From what we've heard Jesus say in the Sermon on the Mount so far, we might not expect money to be where he's going next. He's stirred our hearts with his declaration that we are blessed. He's sparked our imaginations with dreams of being salt and light. He's challenged us with a radical vision of love. And he's reminded us that the true reward we're after can be found in the One who already notices us. Sure, this opposite life seems challenging, but it's also pretty inspiring and motivational!

And then Jesus says, "Okay, now let's talk about money."

Our Money Problem

Imagine that you're sitting in church and the pastor announces, "Next week we're going to begin a new series on finances and generosity." What happens inside you?

Money is a fraught topic for a lot of us, laden with fear, uncertainty, and other emotions. Talking about it triggers an inner dialogue full of tension. We feel threatened when someone presumes to tell us how to feel about our financial resources or what to do with our money. Our instinct is to avoid conversations about money.

But Jesus dives right into this tension and tells us we have a money problem.

Here's the thing: The money problem Jesus addresses is not about a lack of resources. No doubt there were those in the crowd who were poor and lacked necessities. Jesus had compassion on them, and at times, he acted to miraculously provide for them.[4] But Jesus also spent time with people like the rich young ruler, those who had reached a certain threshold of financial security. The money problem Jesus sees isn't about the size of our bank accounts. It's deeper than that. Jesus is concerned with a heart problem.

The truth is, whether we have a little or a lot, each of us is at high risk for heart disease when it comes to money. It's a preexisting condition for being human. Without the proper precautions and treatment, this problem will make us sick, keeping us from fully following Jesus and living in his Kingdom.

Yet, like a patient who resists going to the doctor to avoid hearing a distressing diagnosis, we resist talking about money, possessions, and generosity. Do you feel that resistance in you? Most of us do. And it causes us to ignore the warning signs of our disease.

No one knows our hearts' true condition except us (and God). So let's get honest with ourselves and do a little self-diagnosis—because curing our financial heart disease is critical to experiencing the abundant life Jesus has for us in the Kingdom.

Symptom #1: Accumulation

[Jesus said,] "Do not store up for yourselves treasures on earth, where moths and vermin destroy, and where thieves break in and steal."
MATTHEW 6:19

Do you like to go treasure hunting?

Whether we look for treasures in a clothing store, the Apple store, a bookstore, a thrift store, a home-improvement store, or the store that is open 24/7 on our laptops, we've all experienced the thrill of treasure hunting. Who hasn't had the experience of walking into Target intending to buy ten dollars' worth of toiletries only to emerge thirty minutes later with fifty dollars' worth of merchandise, including two throw pillows and a bouquet of fresh tulips? (This may or may not have happened as I was writing this chapter.)

But possessions alone are not the treasures Jesus is referring to. Treasures have an emotional component: They are objects from which we try to derive joy.

Often, this joy comes to us in the form of *more*. All the shiny things available to us on the earth fuel in us a desire to acquire, and most of us have fed that desire with a constant stream of purchases.

Researchers from the University of California, Los Angeles, visited the homes of typical American families, documented everything found in these living spaces, and concluded that "contemporary U.S. households have more possessions per household than any society in global history."[5] Just look in the corners of your home, your garage, your closets. What do you see? I don't know about you, but I see a lot of objects that I once considered treasures but now, removed from the dopamine rush of shopping, just look like clutter.

The treasures of earth can't deliver the satisfaction we're after. Don't believe me? Just go stand in your closet or your home office or your garage. Identify an object that you were consumed with acquiring a year or two ago. You may still like it. You may even value it. But did it really satisfy the longings in your life? Have you been perfectly content since you bought it? Of course not. We know stuff can't bring us lasting satisfaction. And yet we continue to accumulate it.

This endless consumption is making us sick with debt, disillusionment, and disordered hearts. But there is hope. If you see the symptom of accumulation in your life, take heart: Jesus has given the prescription.

> "Store up for yourselves treasures in heaven, where moths and vermin do not destroy, and where thieves do not break in and steal."
> MATTHEW 6:20

How do you treat the sickness of endless accumulation? By going on a different kind of treasure hunt. Because guess what? The desire within you that you're trying to satisfy through accumulation is not the problem. We all long for a sense of joy, fulfillment, even transcendence. Our problem is that we are fooled over and over into thinking we can find this satisfaction in material stuff. We convince ourselves that the dopamine burst we get from something new and improved will fulfill us. It won't.

It will quickly fade. Only treasures in heaven can deliver the satisfaction we're after.

The phrase *treasures in heaven* might lead us to believe that the fulfillment of our desires is only a future reality. But when Jesus speaks of heaven in the Sermon on the Mount, he's not talking about a place where we'll go after we die but rather the present realm where God dwells and reigns. He's talking about the Kingdom of Heaven—or as we've been calling it, the Kingdom of God. That Kingdom is accessible to us now!

Storing up treasures in heaven means fully investing yourself in the pursuit of intimacy with God and life in his Kingdom. N. T. Wright explains,

> We shouldn't imagine [Jesus] means "don't worry about this life—get ready for the next one." "Heaven" here is where God is right now, and where, if you learn to love and serve God right now, you will have treasure in the present, not just in the future.[6]

The fulfillment of our true desires is available to us, but we won't find it on Amazon. We will only find it in an allegiance to King Jesus and life in his Kingdom.

Accumulation of earthly treasures is a symptom of heart disease. Do you see any warning signs of it in your life?

Symptom #2: Stinginess

[Jesus said,] "The eye is the lamp of the body. If your eyes are healthy, your whole body will be full of light. But if your eyes are

unhealthy, your whole body will be full of darkness. If then the light within you is darkness, how great is that darkness!"
MATTHEW 6:22-23

At first glance, this passage can seem like a departure from the money topic. Jesus has left all talk of treasures behind and now seems to be focused on eyesight. But not so fast. There is some clever wordplay at work here. To more deeply understand what Jesus is saying, we must first "address ancient views of human physiology and eyesight in particular."[7]

In the ancient world, the eye was understood as "a channel for light as it leaves the body," a window between the inside and outside of a person. The common understanding was that "the eye illuminates the light (or lack of light) within the body."[8] Of course, with our modern, scientific understanding of eyesight, we know that the eye instead takes in light. Yet we still recognize the sentiments of the ancient view when we say things like "The eye is the window to the soul."

Jesus uses a common first-century understanding of eyesight to diagnose a heart problem. When Jesus says, "If your eyes are healthy," the word used by Matthew for "healthy" (*haplous*) can imply generosity (in fact, some English versions of the Bible translate the related word—*haplotēs*—as "generosity" in other New Testament passages[9]). Similarly, when Jesus says, "But if your eyes are unhealthy," this notion of a "bad eye" (*ophthalmos ponēros*) can connote a jealous stinginess (see Matthew 20:15).

What Jesus is saying is that what comes out of us reveals what is inside us. If what comes out of us is generosity, we are full of light. If what comes out of us is stinginess, we are full of darkness. Jonathan Pennington writes, "The principle stated most clearly and practically is that one's relationship to money is not a neutral matter but affects and reflects the inner person."[10]

Again, let's do a little self-diagnosis. Do you consider yourself generous with your money? What might your patterns of charitable giving reveal about the condition of your heart?

My parents are my heroes when it comes to generosity. When I was a child, we'd be watching TV in our family room on a typical Saturday evening, and during a commercial break my dad would get up, walk over to his desk, open the upper left drawer, and pull out his checkbook to write the weekly check to our church. He'd put it in the offering envelope our church provided, and sometimes on the following morning, I'd get to be the one to put it in the plate.

As I'm writing this, my dad is ninety-one and struggling with the beginning signs of dementia. A few years ago, when financial numbers became too confusing for him and my mom, I took over managing their accounts. My dad had one request. He wanted to know if he could still write their offering checks himself. That's what mattered to this man about money. Each year when their Social Security payments go up with the slight cost-of-living increase, my mom contacts me to let me know that their budget needs to be adjusted to tithe an extra ten or twenty dollars. This isn't even counting all the random acts of generosity they perform every time they hear about a need in their community or an opportunity to support a student on a mission trip. My parents are not wealthy. They live on a very fixed income. And yet light pours out of them on a regular basis.

And you know what? They are rich in a way stinginess prevents us from becoming. They experience opportunities to give as a privilege, not a threat. I'd be willing to bet they've never disengaged or gotten angry when their church has taught on stewardship and generosity. If they experience frustration, it's because they wish they could give more.

Generosity is a sign of a healthy heart. Stinginess is a symptom of a problem. Do you see any warning signs of that problem in your life?

Symptom #3: Worry

[Jesus said,] "Therefore I tell you, do not worry about your life, what you will eat or drink; or about your body, what you will wear. Is not life more than food, and the body more than clothes?"
MATTHEW 6:25

Jesus' third statement on money is a big one. If you are an American, chances are that you are symptomatic when it comes to financial worry. A survey conducted during a time of economic stability in the US found that "more than half of Americans felt anxious or insecure about money sometimes, often, or all the time."[11]

But let's consider Jesus' statement honestly. In the Sermon, he talks about being worried that you won't have enough to eat or drink, or that you won't have a garment to clothe your nakedness. Have you ever been in that position? Yes, an estimated 12 percent of Americans live in poverty,[12] but I'm making a reasonable guess that if you're reading this book, you don't have a justifiable fear of starvation or public nudity. *Atlantic* columnist Arthur C. Brooks notes, "For millions of people, then, worrying about money is not a reflection of whether their basic needs are being met. In fact, this anxiety reflects deeper concerns that money can't solve."[13]

So what's really underneath this anxiety?[14] Every day we are bombarded with messages that fuel in us a suspicion that we are in danger of missing out. It's the oldest trick in the book. Adam and Eve ignored the abundance available to them, falling for the lie that they lacked the one thing that could bring fulfillment. Our deceiver no longer needs to slither up and whisper to us directly—we constantly feed on these messages ourselves one HGTV show, Apple livestream event, and social media scroll at a time. This can cause us to live in a perpetual state of dissatisfaction. And, like with Adam and Eve, the real tragedy in all this is that we begin to doubt we can trust God's heart.

At the core of our financial worry is a struggle to truly trust God. Jesus is alerting us to emotional and spiritual factors tied to money that rob us of peace and contentment.

Do you, in your heart of hearts, believe that God cares about you?

Do you believe that your well-being matters to him?

Do you believe that he will provide for your needs—mind you, not all your wants, but your true needs?

Listen to how Jesus tries to reason with us:

"Look at the birds of the air; they do not sow or reap or store away in barns, and yet your heavenly Father feeds them. Are you not much more valuable than they? Can any one of you by worrying add a single hour to your life?

"And why do you worry about clothes? See how the flowers of the field grow. They do not labor or spin. Yet I tell you that not even Solomon in all his splendor was dressed like one of these. If that is how God clothes the grass of the field, which is here today and tomorrow is thrown into the fire, will he not much more clothe you—you of little faith? So do not worry, saying, 'What shall we eat?' or 'What shall we drink?' or 'What shall we wear?' For the pagans run after all these things, and your heavenly Father knows that you need them."

MATTHEW 6:26-32

Jesus is saying, "Look at all the evidence of God's loving care! Look at all the proof of his abundant provision!" The evidence that God is trustworthy as a provider is all around you—if you have eyes to see it.

Let's try something together. Bring to mind something tangible with a financial connection that makes you feel dissatisfied. If you can, physically stand in front of that object.

Maybe it is a car that you'd love to trade in for a newer model.

Maybe it is an outdated room in your house that you'd like to remodel.

Maybe it is your closet, where it frequently feels like you have nothing good to wear.

Maybe it is your phone, with a scratch on the screen.

Maybe it is a possession you don't have yet.

Look, and feel your dissatisfaction.

I am sitting in my en suite bathroom. It has a flower wallpaper border that I put up twenty-two years ago. One wall has an unpainted patch where I had to ask a friend to repair a football-sized section of drywall after my shower leaked water. The white linoleum on the floor shows every single piece of dirt and hair. I hate it.

But what if I choose to look at this room through different eyes? Every morning I simply turn a lever and have a plentiful supply of water to make myself feel clean and fresh. The water pressure in my shower is fantastic. (I would buy a house based on the quality of the water pressure in the shower alone.) And, of course, this is my *en suite bathroom*, meaning there are other bathrooms in the house.

Now, don't get me wrong. If I could snap my fingers and have a remodeled bathroom, I'd absolutely do it! But my point is this: Worry is often a matter of perspective. We can choose to focus on the things we lack and our inability to provide them. Or we can focus on the abundance God has already given us and trust him to provide for our real needs moving forward. Gratitude is a great antidote to worry.

Worrying about money is a symptom of a heart problem. If you see it in yourself, it might be a good time to request that your pastor teach on finances and generosity. (Seriously, do it. You'll enjoy the look of shock on your pastor's face.)

HEAR FROM GOD

Lord, I want to hear from you. Come, Holy Spirit. Speak to me and empower me to do what you say. Amen.

Which of the three symptoms of financial heart disease (accumulation, stinginess, and worry) do you see in your life? Ask God to reveal to you what is lying behind the symptom(s). Talk with him about your willingness (or unwillingness) to address this.

What is God saying to you at this moment? What will you do in response?

These three symptoms—accumulation, stinginess, and worry—are indicators of the deeper money problem within our hearts. Jesus describes the problem this way:

> "No one can serve two masters. Either you will hate the one and love the other, or you will be devoted to the one and despise the other. You cannot serve both God and money."
>
> MATTHEW 6:24

Jesus names money as his biggest rival for our allegiance. The ways in which we manage our resources reveal which master has our affection. Or, as Jesus puts it, "where your treasure is, there your heart will be also."[15]

In fact, financial stewardship might be the most objective indicator of spiritual growth and maturity. Think about it. How can you tell if you are growing in your prayer life? How can you quantify an increase in your love for others? How can you measure your ability to extend grace? All these things are part of growing to spiritual maturity, yet it can be hard to recognize your progress. But you *can* evaluate whether you are growing in generosity or not: Look at your bank statements, track what you invest in the Kingdom of God from year to year, and draw some conclusions about your financial priorities.

Do you take Jesus seriously when he names money as his biggest rival for our allegiance? Or do you blow him off? Do you think he's overreacting? If he really is our King, we need to pay attention—because if we don't address the symptoms of accumulation, stinginess, and worry in our lives, there is a pretty good chance we'll be mastered by money. It's difficult to live in the Kingdom of God when you are following a rival king. New Testament scholar Scot McKnight writes, "If the kingdom vision of Jesus doesn't reshape our approach to possessions, then we are not living out the kingdom vision."[16]

The Opposite

Jesus tells us that the opposite way when it comes to money is to "seek first his kingdom and his righteousness."[17] What does this look like? We prioritize the Kingdom of God in our budgets. We practice behaviors that help align our whole being with God's will. We start to realize that generosity isn't something God wants *from* us; it is something he wants *for* us. In the counterintuitive way of Jesus, we flourish not by holding on to what we have but by giving it away.

What if the path to shalom is not in having 10 percent more but in living on 10 percent less?

Returning 10 percent of everything you receive back to God—a spiritual practice called tithing—was established in the Old Testament.[18] As usual, Jesus raises the bar in the New Testament when he praises not the tithers following the letter of the law but a poor widow who gives everything she has.[19] For the first Christ followers, radical generosity was the natural outgrowth of their authentic allegiance to the risen King: "All the believers were one in heart and mind. No one claimed that any of their possessions was their own, but they shared everything they had."[20] Maybe when you have stood face-to-face with Jesus, holding anything back from him feels absurd?

It is hard for most of us to imagine being that free when it comes to money and possessions. But we can take a step in that direction by practicing the tithe.

When I was growing up, my parents modeled tithing, giving 10 percent of their income back to God. It was so normative in my house that I grew up assuming it's just what every person who follows Jesus would naturally do. I tithed off my first Taco Bell paycheck at sixteen years of age, and even when I was making twenty-one thousand dollars a year with no benefits in my midtwenties, it was never an issue for me. I tithed, and God provided for my needs. I tell you that not to boast but to plead with you. If you are a parent, you have no idea what a gift you could give your kids if you live out this area of your allegiance. Not only will they experience it as a normal part of life, but they will also have trust in God's provision solidified at a young age. I am forever grateful to my parents for doing that for me. Yes, I still struggle with some of the symptoms of financial heart disease, in particular the desire to acquire. But

I know my heart is so much healthier than it would have been in this area of money and possessions because of their example. If tithing is a new step for you, it may take you a while to live into it. But commit to it now, and develop a plan for growing into it—and watch God slowly move your heart toward confidence and trust in his care and provision as you give your allegiance to him.

Many of us struggle day after day with the symptoms of our financial heart disease without pursuing the cure. It doesn't have to be that way. Jesus cares enough about our well-being to address money and possessions in his Sermon. He equips us to do the opposite of the world and seek first his Kingdom by beginning to practice generous behaviors. Just like with physical heart disease, tending to financial heart disease will require lifestyle changes—but becoming heart healthy is a much better way to live.

CHAPTER 9

GROWING IN RELATIONAL MATURITY

Matthew 7:1-12

IN 2019, WHEN A TV SERIES called *The Chosen* began releasing episodes about the life and ministry of Jesus, I was a bit skeptical. After all, I've seen enough low-budget Christian media productions to instinctively brace myself for a healthy dose of the cheese factor. But *The Chosen* surprised me. The Jesus this show portrays is loving, intelligent, and whimsical. The compelling nature of his personality draws people to him. He treats them with a kindness and compassion they haven't experienced in their own religious leaders.

The Jesus portrayed in *The Chosen* seems a lot like the Jesus we read about in Scripture. Jesus was at home in his own human skin, and he seemed to create space for others to be at home in theirs too. They didn't feel shamed or shunned in his presence, despite their flaws and failures. I think it is fair to say that Jesus is the most relationally mature person who has ever set foot on planet earth.

When it comes to the disciples, we have no way of knowing whether *The Chosen* portrays their mannerisms and personalities accurately, but I love the way the series helps us imagine them as real human beings in messy, complicated relationships with one another. Perhaps most intriguing is how the show has fleshed out Matthew, the former tax collector who wrote the first Gospel. Watching Matthew as an intelligent yet socially awkward man who followed Jesus around recording what he saw and experienced in his trusty journal makes me smile. Maybe it's because I can imagine myself choosing an evening of recording the day's events in my own journal over socializing with a group of people around a campfire.

Of the Twelve, only Matthew and John compiled narratives about Jesus' life. John's book seems like it is written years after the events it records, serving as both personal reflection and theological summary of who Jesus is and what he came to do. Matthew's book feels like it is written from detailed notes. Matthew wants us to know what was said and what happened as accurately as possible. And, of course, it is in Matthew's version of the story that we find the Sermon on the Mount.

Now remember, Matthew wasn't taking dictation at the time Jesus gave these teachings. He wasn't sitting off to the side like a court reporter with a stenotype machine capturing every word. Matthew may have written down bits and pieces of what he witnessed as he followed his rabbi through the towns and villages of Galilee, Samaria, and Judea. But it would be some years before he, directed by the Holy Spirit, compiled these stories and teachings into the literary work that we know as the Gospel of Matthew.

In fact, there is good reason to believe that what we call the Sermon on the Mount isn't a single sermon at all but rather a collection of Jesus' most important and memorable teachings. Some biblical evidence for this can be found if you look up Matthew 4:23 and Matthew 9:35. These two verses are nearly identical. They both tell of Jesus traveling throughout the region "proclaiming the good news of the kingdom, and healing every disease and sickness." This repetition is a common literary device Matthew employs to signal the beginning and ending of a section of his book. (Remember, in its original form, Matthew's book didn't contain chapter and verse divisions!) What lies between these parallel verses is a summary of Jesus' teachings (Matthew 5–7) and a summary of Jesus' healings (Matthew 8–9). Jewish scholar Amy-Jill Levine concludes, therefore, that "the Sermon on the Mount could easily be retitled 'A Sampling of Jesus's Greatest Teachings.'"[1]

I point all this out because Matthew 7:1-12 can be the most confusing section of the Sermon to interpret. It feels a bit haphazard—Jesus seems to bounce from one topic and illustration to another in rapid succession. But if we keep in mind that the Sermon is most likely a collection of Jesus' teachings, we can ask a different and more helpful question: Why did the Spirit prompt Matthew to compile this group of teachings together?

Let me admit: We can't definitively answer that question. Some scholars see this section, which concludes the main body of teaching in the Sermon, as a collection of several smaller, unrelated teachings that Matthew just wanted to make sure were included. That very well could be true. I'm intrigued by another perspective of this section that considers the way it begins and ends: with a focus on relationships. Did Matthew place these teachings together because he understood that through them, Jesus was giving us a multifaceted picture of what it looks like to develop relational maturity as a Kingdom person?

Growing in the ways of the Kingdom of God is meant to transform us. As we follow Jesus in his opposite way of life, we should expect to find ourselves becoming more and more at home in our own skin, and more and more able to create space for others to be at home in theirs. We should anticipate developing a relational maturity that enables us to live lives of shalom within ourselves *and* with others. Dallas Willard, who does see a relational thread through this section of the Sermon, says that these teachings "illustrate the inner texture of kingdom life with family, friends, co-workers, and 'next door' neighbors. They illustrate the kingdom attitude toward those closest to us."[2] Viewed from this perspective, Jesus' teaching in this section can offer a contrasting view of immaturity and maturity in the way we relate to one another.

As we engage with Jesus' words, let's be honest with ourselves about where we are in the journey of relational transformation. After all, if Jesus were with us in the flesh right now, he would create the space for us to be authentic and vulnerable.

Condemning or Compassionate?

[Jesus said,] "Do not judge, or you too will be judged. For in the same way you judge others, you will be judged, and with the measure you use, it will be measured to you.

"Why do you look at the speck of sawdust in your brother's eye and pay no attention to the plank in your own eye? How can you say to your brother, 'Let me take the speck out of your eye,' when all the time there is a plank in your own eye? You hypocrite, first take the plank out of your own eye, and then you will see clearly to remove the speck from your brother's eye."

MATTHEW 7:1-5

Most of us can be quick to reach a judgment about other people based on their words or actions, their values or beliefs. Be honest with yourself. Can you recognize in yourself a tendency to use specks of sawdust to categorize people as good or bad, as right or wrong, as worthy or unworthy?

Just as in English, the Greek word translated "judge" in the New Testament, *krinō*, has two meanings. It can mean to demonstrate healthy discernment ("I judged that the CEO wasn't telling the truth about the product"; "I judged that this relationship was not a healthy one for me to pursue") or it can mean to sit in a place of superiority to condemn.

Of course, Jesus isn't telling us to avoid wise discernment. In fact, in the conclusion of the Sermon, he'll tell us that it's essential that we practice discernment in whom we choose to follow. But what he *is* addressing here is our tendency to observe the words and actions of others and assume the position of judge. While a functioning society necessitates certain people having this power in the criminal-justice system, too often in our relational encounters *we* put on the robe, grab the gavel, and assume authority that isn't ours.

It's disturbing to me how quickly I can place myself in the position of judge. When I witness a person behaving badly or hear an unfavorable story about them, my instinct can be to mentally throw them into the "bad" bucket. This instinct is especially heightened if their offense directly impacts me. I can effortlessly look past all the planks in my own eye to focus on and condemn the speck in someone else's. I think most of us have this kind of vision when it comes to judging others.

HEAR FROM GOD

Lord, I want to hear from you. Come, Holy Spirit. Speak to me and empower me to do what you say. Amen.

Which person or group of people do you tend to toss into the "bad" bucket? What is going on in your own heart as you think about them? What does this tell you about your own journey of relational transformation?

What is God speaking to you? How will you respond with your actions?

When our discernment crosses over into making judgments that declare people good or bad, we have entered dangerous territory. In effect, by labeling someone bad, we are denying their inherent worth as a human being made in the image of God. We're no longer discerning between right and wrong; we're judging *who* is right and *who* is wrong.

We should note that this tendency to act as judge is the only time Jesus uses the rebuke *You hypocrite* to refer to his own followers. Normally he reserves that nomenclature for the Pharisees and other religious leaders. But here he's warning us, his disciples, that we are telling on ourselves when we assume the authority to condemn.

Something I've noticed about the more mature disciples of Jesus among us: They don't feel the need to condemn. Sure, they may speak out against injustice or wrongdoing, but their words are never laced with personal attacks. When we are aware of our own shortcomings, we may discern the faults of others—but we aren't inclined to assume the role of judge.

Jesus challenges us to be more aware of the plank in our own eye and more concerned with the plank's removal than we are fixated on the speck in someone else's eye. I have the feeling that if we would do what he says, we'd find that our tendency to assume the role of judge would dissipate. Pastor Andy Stanley shares, "The more aware I am of what God has yet to do in me, the less aware I am—and the less consumed I am—by what he has yet to do in the people around me."[3]

And yet Jesus ends this short teaching in a way we might not expect. We might have expected him to end this talk of planks and specks by saying, "So don't point out other people's faults and failures!" Full stop. But that's not what Jesus says. Instead, he tells us *when* and *how* to respond. The relationally mature disciple who lives in awareness of their own shortcomings is able, in turn, to look at the shortcomings of others and respond not with condemnation but with compassion.

Consider, for example, my friend Eric Dorsey. Eric became

a follower of Jesus at the young age of ten. He grew up going to church, was personally involved in ministry, and could never have imagined he'd find himself in prison. Through Eric's own personal experience of incarceration, God grew a desire in his heart to love people whom most in our society have thrown into the "bad" bucket: the men and women in our prisons.

In 2018, Eric joined the staff of Community Christian Church (COMMUNITY) to pioneer a new ministry called Community Freedom.[4] As Eric will tell you, many of the people he ministers to endured adverse childhood experiences and were told (directly or indirectly) that they were bad their entire lives. Many of them internalized this condemnation, and it set the course for their actions and decisions. Few have had people in their lives who have compassionately asked, "What happened to you?" But Eric does this.

Eric told me,

> I know that each of us has the potential to do good or bad things, but our identity is rooted in the fact that God made each of us in his image. I have learned that God's image is best cultivated in an environment of love, belonging, and a compassionate, Christ-centered community. This environment allows the fruit of God's Spirit to grow in us and eventually impact our thoughts, beliefs, and behavior. It's a process that leads to transformation.[5]

Through Community Freedom, our church has planted congregations in three prison facilities in the Chicago area. Eric and his team of volunteers also help transition returning citizens from confinement to freedom once they are released from prison. John,[6] who found his way back to God by participating in Community Freedom services, made it a point after he was released to show up at one of our COMMUNITY services to find Eric. John told him, "I had to come and find you to let you know that I am alive because of the words that you spoke to me. After I was incarcerated, I was suicidal and depressed, but coming to Community Freedom services gave me hope that God could help me turn my life around." John is now reconciled with his parents and working with the Community Freedom reentry team to rebuild his life on his new foundation of faith.

Most of us love these stories of compassion, right? But what about when the offenders are the people we encounter in our everyday lives? What happens when we come across the rude salesperson, the arrogant coworker, the intoxicated neighbor, the ungrateful teenager, or the self-righteous family member? Do we embody compassion in these encounters?

Because relationally mature people see their own sin so clearly, they can feel compassion when confronted with the brokenness of others. And when that compassion is offered consistently and lovingly, it might just open a door for the relationally mature person to help the other person address their sin. The apostle Paul says, "Brothers and sisters, if someone is caught in a sin, you who live by the Spirit should restore that person gently."[7]

The next time you discern something wrong in someone else's life, pay attention to the tendency in your own heart and mind. Do you instinctively move toward condemnation or compassion? If it's the former, it's time to do some plank removal.

Controlling or Empowering?

[Jesus said,] "Do not give dogs what is sacred; do not throw your pearls to pigs. If you do, they may trample them under their feet, and turn and tear you to pieces."

MATTHEW 7:6

This verse is the most confusing and hard-to-interpret verse in the entire Sermon, and it used to make me bristle a bit. I didn't like the thought of Jesus calling people dogs and pigs, especially because some commentators think he is referring to the Gentiles. It just seemed so out of character for him.

But then I came across Dallas Willard's fascinating perspective on this obscure passage. Willard argues that Jesus is not referring to certain classes of people but rather addressing our tendency to throw good things at others without discerning whether we should.[8] The problem with giving pearls to pigs is that the animals cannot digest them. Similarly, when we offer our good thing to a person but they aren't in a place to receive it, they don't obtain nourishment from it. Something good only helps if someone can digest it.

Here's what that might look like:

- You have just made a costly mistake at work, and you are regretting that mistake, feeling horrible. Along comes a coworker with a pearl: "You know what you should have done is . . ."

Now, your coworker might be right. They may be offering you a valid idea. But are you in a place to digest it? No! And therefore, you are not helped.

- You are a teenager, feeling all the angst that comes along with this stage of life, and your parents are constantly throwing pearls of correction at you. They may be giving you good direction, but you only feel frustrated.

- You are an elderly widow who has always been able to take care of yourself, but now your adult child is throwing pearls of instruction at you. They want to take care of you, but you're just feeling helpless and demeaned.

- You just want someone to listen, but your spouse is quick to throw a handful of fix-it pearls at you. They think they're solving your problems, but you're left feeling unseen.

- You are in a spiritual crisis, wrestling with life's big questions, and a friend keeps throwing Bible verses and pithy sayings of Christianese at you. You know they have good intentions, but you feel isolated and unknown.

Think of the last time someone in your life lashed out at you or withdrew from you after you offered them some wisdom.

Could it be that you offered pearls when the other person wasn't in a place to digest them? What you said may have been true. It may have even been biblical. If the interaction led to disconnection rather than connection, however, you may have stepped right into what Jesus is warning against.

As Dallas Willard writes,

> What a picture this is of our efforts to correct and control others by pouring our good things, often truly precious things, upon them—things that they nevertheless simply cannot ingest and use to nourish themselves. Often we do not even listen to them. We "know" without listening. Jesus saw it going on around him all the time, as we do today. And the outcome is usually exactly the same as with the pig and the dog. Our good intentions make little difference. The needy person will finally become angry and attack us. The point is not the waste of the "pearl" but that the person given the pearl is not helped.[9]

What we're really trying to do when we throw our pearls is control others. Maybe we're giving advice because we want to feel competent in the relationship. Maybe we're offering clichés because we're uncomfortable with the other person's emotions. Maybe we're providing easy answers because we're afraid to confront our own doubts. Author Henri Nouwen suggests that control can be a tempting substitute for love: "Maybe it is that power offers an easy substitute for the hard task of love. It seems easier to be God than to love God, easier to control people than to love people."[10]

A relationally maturing disciple of Jesus doesn't feel the need to control other people. Rather, they seek ways to empower people. This kind of relational maturity looks like

- loving and supporting people as they take ownership of their own lives,

- simply being present in the silence with someone who is hurting without trying to fix it, and

- holding space for someone to wrestle with questions and doubts and lovingly supporting them as they work out their own relationship with God.

At some point, one of these people may ask you to share a pearl, and then you can kindly and gently share it. They will have a much better chance of digesting your good thing if they feel empowered to decide where and when they are ready to receive it.

Suspicious or Curious?

[Jesus said,] "Ask and it will be given to you; seek and you will find; knock and the door will be opened to you. For everyone who asks receives; the one who seeks finds; and to the one who knocks, the door will be opened."
MATTHEW 7:7-8

Many people think this passage is about our relationships with God and is talking about prayer, and that very well might be. But in the context of Jesus' other comments on relationship, I also think we're invited to consider how these words *ask*, *seek*, and *knock* contrast with how we often relate to one another as human beings.

How often in our relationships do we think we know everything rather than ask questions?

How often do we assume the worst about someone's intentions instead of seeking understanding?

How often do we dig in our heels and defend our perspective rather than knock on our adversary's door and work through things together?

Just think about the last relational conflict you experienced. When we are butting heads with another person, it's easy to think we know what they're thinking, to assume the worst of them instead of seeking to understand, to dig in our heels instead of striving to work things out. Can you see this inclination in yourself?

We fall into this way of relating to one another because of a problem that's become pervasive in our culture: suspicion. We don't trust one another anymore. We tend to believe the best about ourselves and our intentions but be suspicious about the intentions of others. For example, in his book *Collective Illusions*, author Todd Rose references a study in which over five thousand Americans were asked to define what makes a successful life. They were given these two choices:

A. A person is successful if they have followed their own interests and talents to become the best they can be at what they care about most.
B. A person is successful if they are rich, have a high-profile career, or are well known.

Which would you choose? When answering for themselves, 97 percent of those surveyed chose *A*. But when they were asked what they thought most *other* people would choose, 92 percent of respondents believed that other people would choose option *B*.[11]

Isn't that interesting? Most of us see ourselves as having altruistic qualities while suspecting that others are more self-centered.

I struggle with the temptation to slip into suspicion—especially when I know someone holds different beliefs and values than I hold. My defenses go up, and I start forming arguments in my head to defend myself. Do you do that too?

I'd like to suggest that in this passage about asking, seeking, and knocking, Jesus is inviting us to adopt a different posture in relating to other people. This posture requires the relational maturity to not be threatened—and instead to become curious.

The next time you find yourself at odds with another person, what if—rather than arguing for your point of view—you get curious about theirs and ask questions? Rather than assuming the worst about their intentions, what if you get curious and try to understand where they are coming from? Rather than digging in your heels, what if you get curious and invite them to work together with you toward common ground?

In our polarized world, what might happen if we engage people with a posture of curiosity? Maybe, just maybe, we'll end up finding more open doors.

The Opposite

In our culture, our churches, and our relationships, we all too easily can be people who are condemning, controlling, and suspicious. But relationally mature followers of Jesus, in contrast, are compassionate, empowering, and curious. Becoming relationally mature means choosing the opposite of the way we've been approaching other people.

When we find ourselves not just discerning that something is wrong but ready to condemn another human being as wrong, we can stop ourselves and choose to see that person through the compassionate eyes of Jesus.

When we find ourselves wanting to control another person's actions, beliefs, or emotions, we can stop ourselves and choose to look for ways to be an empowering presence in their lives.

When we find ourselves suspicious of a person's motives, choices, or behaviors, assuming we know everything about them, we can stop ourselves and choose to become curious, ask questions, and try to understand the situation from their perspective.

In fact, at the end of this section of his Sermon on the

Mount, Jesus provides a simplistically brilliant teaching on how to choose the opposite consistently in our relationships:

> "In everything, do to others what you would have them do to you, for this sums up the Law and the Prophets."
> MATTHEW 7:12

This touchstone teaching of Jesus, known as the Golden Rule, truly is brilliant because anyone anywhere can follow it. If you want to know what God would have you to do in any relational situation, all you have to be able to do is identify your own desires.

If you'd want to receive mercy, offer mercy.

If you'd want to be shown respect, offer respect.

If you'd want to be given the benefit of the doubt, offer the benefit of the doubt.

New Testament scholar Scot McKnight says, "If you listen to yourself in all of life, you will be led out of yourself into a life of loving others."[12] Do you want to feel more and more at home in your own skin and more and more able to create space for others to be at home in theirs? Do you want a life of shalom within yourself and a life of shalom with others? Pay attention to yourself. Treat others how you'd like to be treated. And you will grow into a relationally mature person who follows Jesus in his Kingdom way of love.

CHAPTER 10

HEARING AND OBEYING JESUS

Matthew 7:13-23

ONE THING YOU SHOULD KNOW about people in vocational ministry is that we're kind of like the characters on *The Big Bang Theory*—except instead of constantly talking about science every time we're in the same room, pastors will inevitably find ourselves in a theology conversation.

A few summers ago, I went to California to visit some ministry friends, Alex and Hannah, and within a few hours of my arrival, the topic of discipleship came up. I had been working on a teaching series for our church on the topic of moving beyond belief to living as disciples of Jesus. As I shared some of the content I was shaping, Alex interjected, "What is your definition of a disciple?" I stumbled around for a few seconds, regurgitating some of the oft-used phrases at our church. Alex wouldn't have it.

"I think you need to give people a simple definition of what it means to be a disciple," he said. "Something that they can grab hold of and apply in every area of their lives."

He then went on to offer one: "A disciple hears from God and does what he says."

Could it really be that simple?

Over the next several weeks, I pondered Alex's definition. Eventually I came to the conviction that yes—it really *is* that simple.

A disciple is someone who lives in a conversational relationship with God: regularly listening for God and hearing from him every day. Jesus may not be physically walking on earth among us, but he is still present with us through the Holy Spirit.[1] He speaks to us through Scripture, through creation, through people, and through the still, small voice within us. If you are a follower of Jesus, the Holy Spirit is with you; he dwells in you and wants to speak to you.

Yet discipleship doesn't stop with hearing from God. A disciple *also does what God says*. Jesus says, "You are truly my disciples *if you remain faithful to my teachings*"[2] and "Anyone who loves me *will obey my teaching*."[3] Over and over, Jesus reminds us that his disciples don't merely listen; his disciples put into practice what they've heard.

What we do matters.

Belief *and* Behavior

Over the course of my life, the dominant message I've heard proclaimed about Christianity centers on belief.

"Do you believe that Jesus is the Son of God?"
"Do you believe that Jesus died for your sins?"
"Do you believe that Jesus rose again?"

When someone assents to these beliefs, we say that the person has "made a decision for Christ" and is now a follower of Jesus.

Don't misunderstand me: Belief is incredibly important. Jesus himself said, "It is my Father's will that all who see his Son and believe in him should have eternal life."[4] If you don't believe Jesus is who he said he is, don't believe in the atoning work of his death, and don't believe he actually rose from the dead, then there is no reason to put your faith in him. Without belief, Jesus becomes only an ancient version of Captain Kirk or Luke Skywalker, a character whom die-hard fans want to learn trivia about but not someone worthy of real-life allegiance.

Belief matters.

But too often we operate as if it's all that matters.

What we *do* matters too.

It is true that we are saved by grace through faith and not by works,[5] but it is also true that faith without works is dead.[6] We could never do anything to earn our salvation, but the evidence of our salvation should be visible in what we do.

Part of our challenge in following Jesus' teachings is that the modern evangelical Christian culture that elevates decision over discipleship may have seeped into our thinking. Since the days of D. L. Moody and Billy Graham, we've emphasized a decision to receive salvation . . . and often left discipleship as something we hope people will choose afterward. Sometimes I imagine Jesus and Paul standing in our churches in stunned silence as they listen to our altar calls that center on believing a few truths "so that you can go to heaven when you die" as they think, *Really? That's what you got from everything we taught you?*

As author Danielle Strickland writes,

> For far too long we have been preaching a message that faith is a one-time decision that we make with our minds. But one decision is merely the doorway for our whole selves to find faith.[7]

Of course becoming a disciple of Jesus includes an initial decision, but it is so much more than that! Deciding to accept God's grace is how we receive salvation—but this decision propels us into lives of discipleship. As Scot McKnight says, "we are saved by Christ, but Christ saves us into discipleship."[8] Being a disciple means giving King Jesus our full allegiance: reorienting everything in our lives around him and making hundreds of decisions every day to follow in his way and live in the Kingdom of God.

James, the brother of Jesus, warns us of an oversized emphasis on belief: "You believe that there is one God. Good! Even the demons believe that—and shudder."[9] If demons are believers, surely following Jesus involves something beyond belief! Belief is important, but it's not sufficient. What we do matters. And yet some of us get nervous when we begin to stress the importance of behavior in the life of faith.

For some of us, stressing the importance of behavior takes us back to how strict adherence to "the rules" has been misused in our backgrounds. I get it. I grew up with a very behavior-focused understanding of following Jesus and consider myself a bit of a recovering legalist. I can remember trying to convince my Christian roommates in college that we should only be listening to Christian music because it was music that honored God. If that was available, I argued, why should we contaminate ourselves with songs that belonged to the world? (I must have been a barrel of fun to live with.)

Looking back, I can see how I was trying to set parameters for what made someone a good Christian so that I could feel good about myself when I followed my own rules. The only thing that came out of that particular rule, however, is that I now sit in complete ignorance when my peers talk about "the music we grew up listening to." Please don't quiz me on 1980s rock or 1990s hip-hop.

Still, others of us get nervous about stressing the importance of behavior because we believe it smells of works righteousness. "We are saved by grace, not works!" we might protest. And again, that's true! But I think part of the problem is that we view grace and works as opposites. We think we have to choose between them. But I don't believe that's how Jesus, Paul, and first-century Christ followers would have seen it.

To understand the relationship between grace and works, let's reflect on the relationship between the covenant and the law in the Old Testament. All the way back in Genesis, God established a covenant with Abraham.[10] Through this covenant, initiated solely by God and reliant on his faithfulness, God declared that Abraham and his descendants would be his people and that he would be their God. He entered a covenantal relationship with them not because they did anything to deserve the honor but because they were God's chosen people. This is grace.

The law, given multiple centuries later to God's chosen people through Moses,[11] did not set aside the covenant. In Galatians, the apostle Paul reminds us,

> The agreement God made with Abraham could not be canceled 430 years later when God gave the law to Moses. God would be breaking his promise. For if the inheritance could be received by keeping the law, then it would not be the result of accepting God's promise. But God graciously gave it to Abraham as a promise.
>
> GALATIANS 3:17-18, NLT

The law did not replace the covenant. The relationship between God and his chosen people was still grounded in his covenantal grace. The law provided instructions on how people were to live *because* they were his chosen people. Following the law did not *make* them his people; following the law *marked* them as being his people.

In the new covenant, initiated solely by God and established through Jesus' blood,[12] God made a way for all people to become part of his chosen people through faith in Jesus Christ. This is grace. We did nothing to earn it.

Jesus didn't just save us, however; he also taught us how to live in the Kingdom of God. The Sermon on the Mount and all his other teachings provide instructions on how we are to live *because* we are his people. The effort we are to make to obey his teaching is not in conflict with grace. Dallas Willard reminds us, "Grace is not opposed to *effort*, but is opposed to *earning*."[13] We don't *earn* anything through our obedience. Obedience to

Jesus' teachings does not *make* us his people; obedience *marks* us as his people.

Faith and works are not opposites. Belief and behavior aren't in conflict with one another. One belongs to the other. Because we believe, we follow Jesus' teachings. Our obedience embodies our belief. A disciple is someone who hears from God and does what he says.

The Call to Discipleship

The Sermon on the Mount is not a collection of teachings about soteriology, laying out an explanation of how a person is saved. Rather, the Sermon on the Mount is a collection of teachings about discipleship. It's an invitation to follow Jesus and live with him in the Kingdom that doesn't operate like the kingdoms you've always known. As he draws to the end of his Sermon, Jesus is not trying to answer the question *Who is and who isn't saved?* but rather *Who is and who isn't living as my disciple?*

All throughout the Sermon, Jesus has taught us about the counterintuitive, upside-down, opposite way of life in the Kingdom of God, the realm in which God's will reigns, where Christ followers increasingly find ourselves

- desiring blessing for everyone, including the people we don't like;
- decentering ourselves and looking for opportunities to bring out the "God-flavors" and "God-colors" in this world;

- respecting and honoring one another's relationships with God, even when we disagree on how to interpret Scripture;
- following Jesus in his radical way of loving people, including turning the other cheek and loving our enemies;
- living for an audience of One, letting go of the impulse to please and perform for people;
- prioritizing the Kingdom in how we manage money and possessions; and
- addressing the shortcomings in our own lives (instead of pointing the finger at others) as we do for them what we'd want done to us.

After casting a soaring vision for what life in the Kingdom of God is meant to look like, Jesus concludes the Sermon with a set of challenging warnings:

> "Wide is the gate and broad is the road that leads to destruction, and many enter through it."
> MATTHEW 7:13

> "Every tree that does not bear good fruit is cut down and thrown into the fire."
> MATTHEW 7:19

> "Not everyone who says to me, 'Lord, Lord,' will enter the kingdom of heaven."
> MATTHEW 7:21

Because of our emphasis on a one-time salvation decision, these warnings may make us start to panic, wondering, *Am I saved or not?* But remember, that's not the question Jesus is addressing. These are the questions he is asking: *Are you doing what I taught you? Are you living as my disciples in the Kingdom of God?*

Ultimately, the wisdom to live the opposite way of life looks like intentionally choosing the narrow road, discerning whom to follow (and whom not to follow), and committing your allegiance to Jesus as King.

Choose the Narrow Road

[Jesus said,] "Enter through the narrow gate. For wide is the gate and broad is the road that leads to destruction, and many enter through it. But small is the gate and narrow the road that leads to life, and only a few find it."
MATTHEW 7:13-14

Every day, we get to choose which road we will travel: the narrow road or the broad road. Jesus does not beat around the bush about which road he wants us to take.

What is this narrow road? The upside-down, counterintuitive, opposite way of the Kingdom of God. The way of life Jesus has been calling us to all throughout the Sermon. And it's narrow because it is the more difficult way to live.

It's easy to walk the broad road. That's why, as Jesus says, many people travel it. On the broad road, you follow along with the crowd and do whatever you want.

On the broad road, you get to hold grudges.

On the broad road, you get to clap back at your enemies on social media.

On the broad road, you get to live by whatever sexual ethic feels right to you.

On the broad road, you get to hoard your resources for yourself and your family.

On the broad road, you get to justify your obsession with power and success.

I think even many Christians choose this road. But where does it lead? To exactly the place where we find ourselves right now.

Broken relationships.

Divided communities.

Widespread injustice.

Senseless violence.

Crippling fear.

The broad road leads to destruction. We can't really blame the people who don't know Jesus for ending up where we've ended up. But what about us?

The good news is the gate to the narrow road is still open to us. In John's Gospel, Jesus declares, "I am the gate."[14] We find the narrow road through Jesus. We enter through him by repenting of the way we have been walking and instead following him in a new direction. We give our allegiance to Jesus and join him in the ways of his Kingdom. Scot McKnight notes,

> The gate is not just a mild association with Jesus or some kind of general affiliation, but a radical

commitment to Jesus as the one who is King and Lord who shapes all of life for us.[15]

The narrow road is demanding. Jesus makes no apologies for that—because it is the only road that leads to life. This is the road Jesus chose. It is the road we'll find him on. And when we follow this road, we move toward Jesus—and toward shalom. Author Skye Jethani writes,

> We do not take the narrow way because it is easy, or because we long to be different. We do not take it merely because the wide road leads to destruction. We take it because on it we encounter the presence of Jesus.[16]

Ultimately, Jesus is asking us, "Will you follow me or not?" Because whom you choose to follow, whom you give your allegiance to, will determine what road you take and what kind of kingdom you live in.

Discern Whom to Follow

[Jesus said,] "Watch out for false prophets. They come to you in sheep's clothing, but inwardly they are ferocious wolves."
MATTHEW 7:15

A lot of people are leading in the wrong direction. A false prophet is someone who claims to be speaking for God but is not approved by God to be his spokesperson. It could be that the person is sharing false teachings. Jesus doesn't focus here on what the false prophet is saying but on the character of the person's life.

How are we to detect a false prophet? By fruit inspection. The false prophet may be saying all the right words, but none of that matters if there is something rotten in the person's life:

> [Jesus said,] "By their fruit you will recognize them. Do people pick grapes from thornbushes, or figs from thistles? Likewise, every good tree bears good fruit, but a bad tree bears bad fruit."
> MATTHEW 7:16-17

"Examine the fruit of a person's life," Jesus says, "and you will be able to discern whether that person should be trusted as someone to follow." What is the fruit to look for? It's not charisma on a platform. It's not the size of a person's following or the number of books they've sold. It's not the promises they make. The fruit is the Kingdom way Jesus taught and modeled. A genuine spiritual leader will reflect Jesus' character, his words, and his ways. Paul described this fruit as love, joy, peace, patience, kindness, goodness, faithfulness, gentleness, and self-control.[17] If you don't observe these things in the lives of the leaders you are following, alarm bells should be ringing in your ears.

Not everyone who uses religious language is speaking for God.

Not everyone who has a book on a Christian bestsellers list is speaking for God.

Not everyone who quotes a Bible verse is speaking for God.

Not everyone who comes from a well-known Christian family is speaking for God.

Not everyone who holds a position of Christian leadership is speaking for God.

In recent years, we've seen too many people in positions of spiritual authority misuse their influence and power. The pain this has caused for those who have been misled and even abused in these circumstances is heartbreaking and inexcusable. And let's face it—this is one of the reasons the church has such a tarnished reputation in the world right now.

Jesus warns us not to be wooed by people whose success and charismatic personalities are naturally impressive. Instead, we must examine the fruit of their lives to see if they are actually following Jesus in the ways of his Kingdom.

Commit Your Allegiance to Jesus

Ultimately, whether we live Jesus' opposite kind of life comes down to allegiance. Will we truly surrender ourselves to him as King? Or will we give lip service to a set of beliefs and continue to live for our own kingdoms?

Jesus says,

> "Not everyone who says to me, 'Lord, Lord,' will enter the kingdom of heaven, but only the one who does the will of my Father who is in heaven. Many will say to me on that day, 'Lord, Lord, did we not prophesy in your name and in your name drive out demons and

in your name perform many miracles?' Then I will tell them plainly, 'I never knew you. Away from me, you evildoers!'"

MATTHEW 7:21-23

Have you ever known someone who has pretended to be someone they were not? One of my favorite imposter stories is about a college student named Danny Foley, who hatched a scheme to be part of the University of Virginia's basketball team in a big championship game against Duke. Danny noticed that all the team's assistant coaches wore the same suit with a bright orange tie. So the night before the game, he went to Walmart and found everything he needed to match the outfit. The next day, he bought a thirty-dollar nosebleed seat and made his move during one of the TV time-outs. He confidently walked past an usher and onto the court and joined the Virginia huddle as he watched the coach draw up a play.

Even better, when Virginia won the championship, Danny joined the team in the handshake line. He shook hands with Duke's legendary coach, Coach K. There are photos from the end of the game of Danny smiling in the confetti-covered arena, wearing a championship T-shirt over his suit.

Of course, eventually a member of Virginia's coaching staff noticed him, and Danny had to quickly jump a railing in the auditorium to disappear into the crowd.[18] This is the way these stories end. The imposter is always found out.

The difference between Danny and the people Jesus references in his Sermon is that the latter don't seem to realize that they are imposters. We must soberly recognize that in this passage Jesus is not talking about atheists or those who have rejected God. He's not talking about people who fake their way onto a church-leadership team or deliberately prey on the good-heartedness of those in the church for financial gain. He's talking about people who think they are following Jesus but really aren't.

The key to understanding this section of the Sermon is in the word *evildoers*. This English word translates a Greek phrase that means "you who practice lawlessness." Jesus is saying that there are those who claim to be his followers who have never really given him their allegiance as King. They don't follow his teachings; they live by their own rules. They may intellectually believe in him, but they continue to do whatever they want, living as lords of their own lives. The relationship between that kind of person and Jesus doesn't really exist.

Imagine a man who marries a woman, making a vow at the altar and saying, "I love you," but whose life in the days and years that follow show nothing that reflects his commitment. He spends all his free time pursuing his own hobbies. He never considers his wife's interests when he makes decisions. He doesn't lift a finger to help around the house. He shows his wife no affection. If you were to ask him, "Do you love her?" he might reply, "Of course I do! I said so on our wedding day!" But the evidence of his actions doesn't validate his words.

The person Jesus is describing in this section is someone who claims to love Jesus but whose life shows no actual evidence of following him. God is not fooled, even if we fool ourselves. As God himself said in the Old Testament book of 1 Samuel, "the Lord does not look at the things people look at. People look at the outward appearance, but the LORD looks at the heart."[19] You can't will your way into the Kingdom of God.

Jesus isn't trying to frighten us into questioning our salvation. After all, he knows that we're going to mess up. His love for us will never waver, and his grace will never run out. Jesus *is* issuing a warning, however. He is challenging those whose walk doesn't match their talk. His intention in these verses is to shake us up so that we can repent and become genuine disciples.

What we do matters. True disciples hear from him and do what he says.

Empowered for Obedience

Sometimes people will ask me, "Is discipleship, then, just about trying harder to be good?" And I understand why people wonder that. We can move beyond belief and into behavior modification far too easily.

Jesus doesn't just call us to follow him in his Kingdom way and then leave us to muster up the willpower to obey. No—he calls us, and then he empowers us. He is present with us in the person of the Holy Spirit. "You are in me, and I am in you," Jesus says.[20] If you are a follower of Jesus, you have everything you need to live the life Jesus calls you to through the power of the Holy Spirit living within you.

After all, that's how Jesus lived in the Kingdom. Don't forget—Jesus became one of us.

Because we know he is God, many of us have a hard time believing that Jesus is really like us. We can tend to have a superhuman view of Jesus' humanity. New Testament scholar Craig Evans says,

> It's almost as though a lot of Christians think of Jesus as God wearing a human mask. He's sort of faking it, pretending to be human. He pretends to perspire, his stomach only appears to gurgle because, of course, he's not really hungry. In fact, he doesn't really need to eat. So Jesus is the bionic Son of God who isn't really human.[21]

But there is a real problem with seeing Jesus this way. How could we be expected to live the way he lived if he didn't really experience the limitations and challenges that come with being human? How could it be realistic for us to become like him and do the things he did if he was holding the "God card" in his back pocket the whole time he walked on this earth? Author Greg Haugh explains that "it would be like Superman asking us to follow him and fly like he does, but without giving us any superpowers."[22]

The New Testament doesn't teach this superhuman view of Jesus' humanity. Instead, what we find in the Gospels and the New Testament letters is a Jesus who emptied himself of his divine glory, knowledge, and power to become one of us.[23] Jesus took on humanity with all its challenges and limitations.

And yet we know that Jesus was able to do something that none of us has been able to do: live a life without sin.[24] And not only that, but Jesus did extraordinary things. He lived a life of purpose and was able to transcend normal human limitations. He modeled the shalom life that he came to bring.

So how did he do it? Jesus lived his human life fully dependent on the Holy Spirit.

The late Wheaton College professor Gerald Hawthorne explains,

> The Holy Spirit was the divine power by which Jesus overcame his human limitations [such as being limited in knowledge and bound by physical space and human strength], rose above his human weakness, and won out over his human mortality.[25]

Jesus modeled how to live in the Kingdom of God through the presence and power of the Holy Spirit. And here is where everything gets mind-blowing: The same Holy Spirit who empowered Jesus is present and available to you and to me. The Holy Spirit equips us to hear from God and do what he says.

Think of your ability to live life in the Kingdom of God like a balloon. If you fill a balloon with your breath, the only way to keep it in the air is to continually smack it upward. That's how we often try to keep ourselves motivated to follow Jesus. We repeatedly "hit" ourselves (or require others to "hit" us) so that we'll "Stop doing this!" or "Start doing that!" or "Read the Bible!" or "Be more generous!" We might be able to keep up this way of living for a while. But let's be honest—this is an exhausting way to live.

But there's another way to keep a balloon afloat: to fill it with helium. Our lives and efforts are meant to be empowered by a supernatural filling of the Holy Spirit, who keeps us soaring spiritually. You have him in you! All who follow Jesus have the Spirit of power within them. How freeing (and refreshing) to realize that the Kingdom life is not fueled by our best efforts but rather by the Spirit of God in us.

The Opposite

Yet many of us live our daily lives independent of the power available to us.

Let's say a man buys a weight bench to do some strength training. Three months later, he takes it back to the store and complains to the clerk that it didn't work. "I didn't grow any muscles," he protests.

The clerk asks, "What was the problem? Did you not have the right weights? Did it not work properly?"

The man responds, "I don't know. I never used it. I just know I don't feel any stronger, so I am done with it."

Isn't this how some of us treat the Holy Spirit? Because we don't live in a daily partnership with the Spirit, we're not experiencing transformation. Living by this power is not a one-and-done decision. Nor is the Holy Spirit a genie in a bottle you only call upon in dire circumstances. If we're going to live in the Kingdom, we must regularly and consistently partner with the Spirit.

What might happen in our lives if we paused every day, several times a day, to pray the simple prayer I have encouraged you to pause and pray in every chapter of this book:

Lord, I want to hear from you. Come, Holy Spirit. Speak to me and empower me to do what you say. Amen.

Hearing from God and doing what he says is the key to living the opposite way of life in the Kingdom of God, and the Spirit wants to empower you to live this life.

- When a relational conflict arises, a disciple asks, *What is God saying to me about this conflict?* and then, empowered by the Spirit, *does what God says.*

- When presented with a need in the world, a disciple asks, *What is God saying to me in this situation?* and then, empowered by the Spirit, *does what God says.*

- When encountering a person who holds contrary beliefs, a disciple asks, *What is God saying to me about how I should treat this person?* and then, empowered by the Spirit, *does what God says.*

- When wounded by a hurtful or wrong action, a disciple asks, *What is God saying I should do in response?* and then, empowered by the Spirit, *does what God says.*

- When pursuing spiritual growth, a disciple asks, *What is God saying my next step should be?* and then, empowered by the Spirit, *does what God says.*

If we, as Christians, would follow this simple way in the small decisions and the big ones, in our daily interactions, in how we choose to spend our time and our money, in all of life, we would find ourselves living in the realm in which what

God wants done is done. We would be partnering with God in bringing more of his Kingdom to earth.

The Sermon on the Mount is a gift to us as followers of Jesus. Through it, we have heard from God. If we internalize the teachings in the Sermon, I believe the Spirit will use them to guide us to live Jesus' opposite way of life.

HEAR FROM GOD

Lord, I want to hear from you. Come, Holy Spirit. Speak to me and empower me to do what you say. Amen.

Pause right now, open your Bible to Matthew 5–7, and read through the entire Sermon on the Mount in one sitting.

Ask God to reveal to you, through Scripture and through his Holy Spirit within you, if there is a teaching of Jesus' that you have heard but are not putting into practice.

What did God say to you as you read? Will you do what he said?

I believe doing the opposite will bring shalom:

- *Shalom to our relationships.* The counterintuitive way of Jesus will help us mend relationships without compromising what we believe. It will bring healing to the relational rifts that grieve us.

- *Shalom to our souls.* Instead of living riddled with fear or anxiety or anger over what is happening in our world, we will live with a quiet confidence that Jesus is on his throne and the Kingdom is not shaken. We will let go of the responsibility for burdens that are not ours to bear. We will let the Son set us free.[26]

- *Shalom to our world.* If we, as followers of Jesus, choose to do the opposite, we will restore our credibility to the watching world. We will make the difference we long to make. We will help people find their way back to God and together bring more of his Kingdom to earth.

Jesus has a vision that leads to shalom. It's his counterintuitive, upside-down, opposite Kingdom way of life. But we will only find it if we do more than hear him—we must do what he says. After all, Jesus' invitation to his first disciples wasn't just "Believe me." It was "Follow me."[27]

Will you?

Epilogue

Matthew 7:24-29

HAVE YOU EVER WATCHED A MOVIE in a movie theater and when it was over felt like you needed a minute before you'd be able to stand up and leave? Not because your leg fell asleep but because the magnitude of what you just witnessed was so overwhelming that while the credits rolled you sat immobilized in your chair.

I wonder if that is how the crowd on that hillside in Galilee felt as Jesus concluded his Sermon. Matthew tells us,

> When Jesus had finished saying these things, the crowds were amazed at his teaching, because he taught as one who had authority, and not as their teachers of the law.
> MATTHEW 7:28-29

Put yourself back in their shoes, sitting on that sloping terrain, trying to grasp the truth that you are blessed, wrestling with the audacious call to love your enemies, daring yourself to embrace the inspirational challenge that you were created to shine like a light in this world. Imagine Jesus' final words in the Sermon ringing in your ears:

> "Therefore everyone who hears these words of mine and puts them into practice is like a wise man who built his house on the rock. The rain came down, the streams rose, and the winds blew and beat against that house; yet it did not fall, because it had its foundation on the rock. But everyone who hears these words of mine and does not put them into practice is like a foolish man who built his house on sand. The rain came down, the streams rose, and the winds blew and beat against that house, and it fell with a great crash."
> MATTHEW 7:24-27

When we read this parable, we might think that the man who built his house on the rock represents Christians and that the man who built his house on the sand represents non-Christians, but that's not what Jesus is saying. Both houses, on the surface, appear the same. They represent two kinds of Christians. Pastor John Stott notes, "Both read the Bible, go to church and listen to sermons. The reason you cannot tell the difference between them is that the deep foundations of their lives are hidden from view."[1]

However, Jesus says, a time will come when the foundation will be revealed.

If we look around our world, our neighborhoods, and even our families and our churches, a lot has been revealed. There are piles of rubble everywhere. Splintered relationships. Fractured communities. Shattered systems. Collapsed institutions.

We can come up with many explanations for why we have ended up here, and there probably isn't any singular reason. But we may have more in common with the foolish man than we'd like to admit. We have heard from Jesus, but too often we have not done what he said.

In this broken world, we will always have trouble.[2] And not everything hard we go through is connected to our own actions. But I wonder how many times we stand in the middle of the rubble because we fail to take the teachings of Jesus seriously. We ignore what he says. We might discover a correlation between our disobedience and our difficulties if we start paying attention. Ask yourself:

- *What might be different in my relationships if I followed Jesus' wisdom to "do to others what you would have them do to you"?*[3]

- *What might be different in my finances if I followed Jesus' call to "store up . . . treasures in heaven" rather than on earth?*[4]

- *What might be different in our world if all of us who call ourselves Christians learned Jesus' upside-down way of loving our enemies and praying for those who persecute us?*[5]

I believe a lot would change.

We can continue to build in the ways we've been building,

or we can choose a different way. We can choose the opposite way of life Jesus is inviting us to in his Sermon.

Back on that hillside, as you hear the people around you expressing their awe, you find yourself wondering,

- *What if every counterintuitive decision Jesus calls me to will lead me to where I truly want to be?*
- *What might happen if I choose his opposite way of life?*

There is only one way to find out the answers to those questions.

And your response is primarily a response to a person—Jesus.

After all, it wasn't only the content of Jesus' Sermon that amazed the people; it was his authority. They knew they were in the presence of Someone who was unlike anyone they'd ever seen. Your response to the Sermon is not primarily a response to what he taught but a response to Jesus himself.

My hope and prayer as we have journeyed through the Sermon together is that you've encountered Jesus and found him irresistible. Discipleship is about living a life of devotion to Jesus. It's about loving Jesus more than anything this world has to offer. It's about giving your full allegiance to him.

Jesus is the truth you have been searching for.

Jesus is the way to a hope-filled future.

Jesus is the life you long for. Wholeness, healing, and freedom can only be found in him.

So choose Jesus. Once you discover life in his upside-down, counterintuitive Kingdom, you won't want to choose any other way.

Acknowledgments

THE AMOUNT OF SUPPORT I HAVE RECEIVED while writing my first book has been meaningful and humbling. My heart is full of gratitude.

To the people of Community Christian Church: At the time of writing, I have had the privilege of serving with you for twenty-three years. Thank you for all the love, encouragement, and support you have shown me as we have journeyed together. My deepest prayer for you is that your hearts will be inseparably attached to Jesus.

To the staff at COMMUNITY: You are family to me. I love being on this team with you and am grateful for all the grace and support you give me. Special thanks to all who serve on the teaching team that I am privileged to lead. We are better together, and you have helped shape and influence many of the thoughts I've shared in this book.

To all my friends, family, and ministry peers who have shared in my excitement about this book and cheered me on: I am profoundly grateful. Your willingness to support me in my writing journey has been so uplifting. Special thanks to my dear friend Katie Purdy, who walked beside me, prayed for me, and encouraged me every step along the way. Forever grateful for you.

To Bette Dickinson, Dave Ferguson, Aubrey Sampson, and Eddie Yoon: I am blessed to have experienced authors in my life who were willing to share their expertise, wisdom, and connections with me as

I began to wade into the waters of publishing. Thank you for helping me along the way!

To Eric Bramlett, Rodrigo Cano, Amy Ciesniewski, Lori Krueger, and Patrick O'Connell: Thank you for reading the first draft of my manuscript. Your encouragement, support, and feedback helped make this book what it became. Thank you, friends.

To Caitlyn Carlson, Dave Zimmerman, and the teams at NavPress and Tyndale: From the moment Caitlyn and I first connected, I sensed God was up to something. Our partnership in this book feels divinely orchestrated, and as a first-time author, I'm grateful to have walked this journey with such kind, supportive, talented people.

Finally, to Mom, Dad, Laurie, Jer, Andrew, and Joe: I love our little family, and I will never take for granted how blessed we are to be a family of shared faith. "Thank you" feels inadequate to express my gratitude for all your love, encouragement, and support. I treasure you.

Discussion Guide

WHEN JESUS DELIVERED THE SERMON ON THE MOUNT, it was a group experience. Plural pronouns appear throughout the text. No doubt after the people heard Jesus' teachings, they discussed, debated, and wrestled with his words together. We'd encourage you to do the same with a small group or friend as you engage with the Sermon by reading *Choosing the Opposite*.

The following discussion guide can be used in a small-group gathering after every person has had the opportunity to read the chapter. If you are reading *Choosing the Opposite* on your own, we'd encourage you to use these discussion questions as prompts for journaling and then invite a friend to coffee to share what impacted you most from the book. We hope this discussion guide will help you hear from God so that you can do what he says.

Chapter 1 | The Opposite

1. When you go to your favorite restaurant, do you order the same thing every time or mix it up on each visit? Why do you think you do this?

2. Have you ever tried doing the opposite of your natural instinct in a situation? What was the outcome, and what did you learn from it?

3. Can you think of any biblical characters who did the opposite of what was expected and experienced significant change?

Take ten or fifteen minutes and read Matthew 5, 6, and 7 out loud.

4. What phrases, verses, or passages stick out to you from Jesus' Sermon? Why do you think those words grab your attention?

5. What are some natural instincts or cultural influences that might conflict with the teachings of Jesus?

6. How do you see the current culture wars affecting your personal relationships and your spiritual life?

7. Discuss a relationship in your life that is strained. What would you like to be true of that relationship in the future?

8. On a scale of 1 to 10, with 1 being *resistant* and 10 being *ready*, how eager do you feel to be challenged to an opposite kind of life?

Chapter 2 | Thinking Upside Down

1. When presented with new ideas, do you tend to be trusting and easily persuaded or cautious and skeptical? Why do you think that is?

Read Matthew 5:1-12.

2. Tammy writes, "The Beatitudes aren't statements telling us what to do; they are observations of what is. Jesus is looking into the faces of worn-out and weary people sitting on a hillside and announcing to them: 'Wherever you find yourself, whatever you are going through, you are blessed!'" What does it mean to you that the Beatitudes are not virtues to be achieved but blessings to be received? How does this change your perception of the teachings?

3. How do the Beatitudes challenge the cultural and societal norms of both Jesus' time and our time? Can you identify any specific cultural patterns today that the Beatitudes contradict?

4. Reflect on a time when you felt like a type of person Jesus describes in the Beatitudes. How does Jesus' message of blessing speak to that experience?

5. In this chapter, Tammy discusses the resistance we can feel to bless those we struggle to like. What groups do you struggle to bless?

6. Our culture influences us to condemn those who differ from us on political and social issues. How can we

approach political and social issues through a Kingdom lens rather than a partisan one? What would it look like to bless those we disagree with rather than curse them?

7. Jesus acknowledges the persecution his followers will face (Matthew 5:11-12). How should we respond when we face opposition?

Read Romans 12:1-2.

8. Paul challenges us to be transformed by the renewing of our minds. How can we practically engage in this transformation to learn to think like Jesus thinks?

Chapter 3 | Choosing Kingdoms

1. Have you ever experienced jet lag? How did it affect your ability to engage with your surroundings and activities?

2. How does the metaphor of jet lag help you understand the challenge of adjusting to the reality of following Jesus?

Read Matthew 4:12-17.

3. Jesus began his public ministry by announcing that the Kingdom had come near. How would you define *the Kingdom of God*?

4. The Kingdom of God conflicts with the kingdoms of this world. Which kingdoms of this world do you find

yourself most attached to? How do these attachments conflict with living in the Kingdom of God?

5. Repentance is an intentional choice to change direction. Share an example of a time you experienced this in your own life.

Read Matthew 4:18-22.

6. Jesus invites us to be his disciples, people who follow him and experience life in his Kingdom. What does giving your allegiance to Jesus look like in practical, everyday terms?

7. Jesus taught us to pray, "Your kingdom come, your will be done, on earth as it is in heaven" (Matthew 6:10). How can you actively participate in bringing more of God's Kingdom to earth in your community?

8. What are some challenges you face in aligning your life with the Kingdom of God? How can Christ followers support and encourage each other to stay committed to following Jesus and living out his teachings?

Chapter 4 | Chasing Grander Dreams

1. When you were a kid, what did you want to be when you grew up? How do your childhood dreams compare to the reality of your adult life?

2. In what ways do you feel a longing for significance in your life?

Jesus calls us, his disciples, to play a significant role in his Kingdom. We are to be "the salt of the earth" and "the light of the world." Read Matthew 5:13-16.

3. Reflect on this statement: "Salt and light aren't meant to be the center of attention." How does this change your understanding of what it means to play a significant role in the Kingdom of God?

4. Can you think of a time when you let the desire for control or recognition or comfort or success overshadow your call to be salt and light? How did that impact your witness?

5. This chapter mentions the communal nature of Jesus' pronouncement. Together we are the salt of the earth. Together we are the light of the world. How does this challenge our individualistic culture? How can we better embody this communal vision in our church community?

6. What are some ways we as a Christian community may have diminished our influence in the world? How can we work to restore that influence in a Christlike manner?

7. How can we practically live out our calling to be salt and light in our daily lives, especially in culturally polarized situations?

8. The chapter ends with a call to live for a bigger dream, focusing on making Jesus and his Kingdom known. What steps can you take to align your life more closely with this vision?

Chapter 5 | Living the Scriptures

1. Name a book, movie, or song you enjoy that other people can't stand (or something other people enjoy that you can't stand).

Jesus and his opponents butted heads over Scripture. They valued the teachings found in the Law and the Prophets, but they differed on how to interpret them. Read Matthew 5:17-20.

2. Why do you think Scripture held such importance for Jesus in his teachings and ministry? How much (or how little) does Scripture impact your daily life right now?

3. The Pharisees often accused Jesus of breaking the law. How did Jesus' interpretation of the law differ from that of the Pharisees, and what can we learn from this?

4. Tammy writes, "Where we often go wrong is in the way we treat people who disagree with our convictions and interpretations. Sometimes we angrily condemn them, mistreat them, and make pronouncements or private judgments about their lives and eternal destination. Sometimes we label them with ugly terms, assume we know their motivations, and set ourselves up as better and more enlightened than them." Where do you see these tendencies in your own life or Christian community when it comes to scriptural disagreements?

5. Jesus calls for a righteousness that surpasses that of the Pharisees. How would you define this greater righteousness? How can we strive to embody it in our own lives?

Read Matthew 22:34-40.

6. Jesus emphasizes that all Scripture hangs on the commandments to love God and to love others. How can this understanding shape our approach to interpreting and applying Scripture?

7. Reflect on a time when engaging with Scripture led to a significant change in your heart or behavior. How can we ensure our Bible study leads to genuine transformation rather than mere knowledge acquisition?

8. Debates around controversial topics are swirling in our modern culture. How can we navigate these difficult conversations while embodying the love and righteousness Jesus calls us to?

Chapter 6 | Loving Radically

1. Do you tend to have the perfect comeback in the heat of an argument, or do you typically think of the perfect comeback too late? How does your typical response make you feel?

In Matthew 5:17-20, Jesus talks about surpassing the righteousness of the Pharisees. In Matthew 5:21-48, he presents six practical examples to illustrate this "greater righteousness." Read Matthew 5:21-48.

2. Why do you think Jesus considers anger and contempt as serious as murder (Matthew 5:21-22)? Why do you think reconciliation is so crucial in the Kingdom of God (Matthew 5:23-26)?

3. Jesus calls us to refuse to objectify others (Matthew 5:27-30). What are some societal or cultural norms that challenge our ability to maintain this respect? How can we cultivate a habit of seeing every person with radical respect?

4. Jesus' teaching on divorce highlights standing with the vulnerable (Matthew 5:31-32). What might radical solidarity with the vulnerable look like in your community?

5. Jesus calls us to speak to one another with truth and integrity (Matthew 5:33-37). Why is radical transparency important in our relationships, and how can we practice it?

6. Jesus teaches to turn the other cheek and go the extra mile (Matthew 5:38-42). What are some modern-day situations where this principle can be applied?

7. Jesus teaches us to love our enemies (Matthew 5:43-48). How can we overcome the instinct to categorize and dismiss certain people as "bad"?

8. Tammy writes, "We shouldn't view these examples simply as rules to follow. They don't address every situation and

circumstance in which we'll find ourselves. But taken together, they begin to show us how a Kingdom person thinks and acts in their relationships with others." How can you apply what you've learned through these examples to help you in a situation you are currently facing?

Chapter 7 | Performing for the Right Audience

1. Before diving into Scripture, take out your phone and take a selfie with an expression on your face that reveals your current mood (e.g., happy, frustrated, tired, excited, sad). Show your picture to others in the group and see if they can guess how you are feeling by viewing your picture.

    If you are doing this study on your own, look at several pictures of yourself stored on your phone. Can you tell what you were feeling at the time by looking at your expression?

2. Whose opinion of you mattered the most when you were a child or teen?

In Matthew 6:1-18, Jesus cautions us about living our lives "to be seen by others." Read the passage.

3. Why do you think our desire to be seen and affirmed by others is so strong? How can this desire lead us astray in different aspects of our lives, such as work, relationships, or social media?

4. Jesus describes a hypocrite as someone who does the right things with the wrong motives. Why is this type of hypocrisy particularly dangerous?

5. How does seeking the approval of others compromise our allegiance to Jesus? Can you share a time when you felt torn between pleasing people and following Jesus?

6. How does it make you feel to know that God notices you?

7. Why is it important to prioritize God's recognition over human approval? How can we cultivate a mindset that values God's opinion more than that of others?

8. Which line in the Lord's Prayer could be most helpful to you right now as you learn to live for an audience of One?

Chapter 8 | Prioritizing the Kingdom

1. How did your family of origin engage in conversations about money? How comfortable are you talking about money now?

Jesus often talked about money and possessions. Read Matthew 6:19-34.

2. Scholar Jonathan Pennington writes that "one's relationship to money is not a neutral matter but affects and reflects the inner person."[1] How do you react to

this idea? Do you believe your financial habits reveal something about your heart? Why or why not?

3. Reflect on your own life: In what ways do you see the accumulation of material possessions affecting your spiritual well-being and relationship with God?

4. What are some common obstacles that prevent people from being generous? Have you personally experienced any of these challenges? How can we overcome them?

5. How do societal messages and media contribute to our tendencies to worry about material possessions and financial security? How can we guard ourselves against these influences?

6. Reflect on Matthew 6:24, where Jesus says, "You cannot serve both God and money." What are some practical examples in your life where you see the tension between following Jesus and pursuing wealth or financial security?

7. Tammy shares a personal story about her parents' generosity despite having limited financial resources. Who are your role models when it comes to generosity? What characteristics of their generosity inspire you?

8. What does it mean practically to "seek first his kingdom and his righteousness" (Matthew 6:33) in the context of your financial decisions and priorities? What next step can you take to align your financial practices with God's Kingdom values?

DISCUSSION GUIDE

Chapter 9 | Growing in Relational Maturity

1. Describe your best friend (either when you were a kid or now as an adult). What qualities does that person have that you value in a friend?

Read Matthew 7:1-12 through a relational lens to see what these verses are telling us about becoming a relationally mature person.

2. Reflecting on 7:1-5, can you identify areas in your life where you have been quick to judge a speck in someone else's eye while ignoring a plank in your own?

3. How does Jesus' teaching on condemnation and compassion challenge prevalent attitudes today, such as cancel culture? How can the church model a different approach, rooted in grace and restoration?

4. What was your first impression upon hearing or reading Matthew 7:6 ("Do not give dogs what is sacred; do not throw your pearls to pigs")? How has your understanding of this verse evolved after considering Dallas Willard's interpretation?

5. Can you recall a time when you offered advice or wisdom to someone with good intentions but it led to disconnection or conflict instead of understanding or connection? What could you have done differently based on Willard's insights?

6. In today's culture, why do you think suspicion toward others has become so prevalent? How does this suspicion affect our ability to build meaningful relationships?

7. Think of a current relationship where suspicion or misunderstanding exists. How could you apply Jesus' teaching of asking, seeking, and knocking (Matthew 7:7-8) to improve understanding and connection in that relationship?

8. What next step can you take to grow as a relationally mature Kingdom person? How might embracing Jesus' Golden Rule (Matthew 7:12) contribute to this growth?

Chapter 10 | Hearing and Obeying Jesus

1. How does the definition of *disciple* Tammy presented ("A disciple is someone who hears from God and does what he says") challenge or affirm your current understanding of discipleship?

2. How has modern Christianity's emphasis on belief shaped your own spiritual journey? Have you ever felt the disconnect between "making a decision for Christ" and ongoing obedience to the teachings of Jesus (either in your own life or in the lives of those around you)?

Jesus drives home the importance of obeying his teachings in the conclusion of the Sermon on the Mount. Read Matthew 7:13-29.

3. Jesus says that few people travel the narrow road (Matthew 7:13-14). What are some personal or societal challenges a disciple will face when trying to follow Jesus in his opposite, counterintuitive way?

4. How can the principles Jesus teaches help us navigate the complexities of choosing whom to trust and follow in a digital age filled with information and influencers? Reflect on Matthew 7:15-20 to help you answer this question.

5. What distinguishes an imposter who claims allegiance to Jesus from a genuine disciple? How can we avoid falling into the trap of mere lip service to Jesus as King? See Matthew 7:21-23.

6. What does it mean practically to be empowered by the Holy Spirit in our daily lives? How is this different from trying to live in the Kingdom of God through mere human effort?

7. What are some common challenges or obstacles we face in maintaining a daily partnership with the Holy Spirit? How can we overcome these challenges?

8. Jesus invites us to live a counterintuitive, upside-down Kingdom life. What are some specific areas in your life where you sense God calling you to do the opposite of what culture or your own instincts dictate? How can the group pray and support you in responding to this call? If you are doing this study on your own, who could you ask to pray for you and support you as you respond to this call?

Notes

CHAPTER 1 | THE OPPOSITE
1. *Seinfeld*, season 5, episode 22, "The Opposite," written by Larry David, Jerry Seinfeld, and Andy Cowan, directed by Tom Cherones, aired May 19, 1994, on NBC.
2. Dallas Willard, *The Divine Conspiracy: Rediscovering Our Hidden Life in God* (San Francisco: HarperSanFrancisco, 1998), 140.
3. Jonathan T. Pennington, *The Sermon on the Mount and Human Flourishing: A Theological Commentary* (Grand Rapids: Baker Academic, 2017), 159.
4. John 8:36.

CHAPTER 2 | THINKING UPSIDE DOWN
1. Warren Carter, "Power and Identities," in *Preaching the Sermon on the Mount: The World It Imagines*, ed. David Fleer and Dave Bland (St. Louis: Chalice Press, 2007), 21.
2. Jonathan T. Pennington, *The Sermon on the Mount and Human Flourishing: A Theological Commentary* (Grand Rapids: Baker Academic, 2017), 144.
3. John 6:37.
4. Carter, "Power and Identities," 21.
5. N. T. Wright, *Paul for Everyone: Romans, Part 2: Chapters 9–16* (Louisville, KY: Westminster John Knox Press, 2004), 69.
6. John 6:60.
7. Matthew 16:24-25.
8. John 6:66.

CHAPTER 3 | CHOOSING KINGDOMS
1. *Kingdom of Heaven* and *Kingdom of God* mean the same thing. They can be used interchangeably.

2. Amy-Jill Levine, *The Sermon on the Mount: A Beginner's Guide to the Kingdom of Heaven* (Nashville: Abingdon Press, 2020), xi–xii.
3. Dallas Willard, *The Divine Conspiracy: Rediscovering Our Hidden Life in God* (San Francisco: HarperSanFrancisco, 1998), 25.
4. Cornelius Plantinga Jr., *Not the Way It's Supposed to Be: A Breviary of Sin* (Grand Rapids: Eerdmans, 1996), 10.
5. John 10:10.
6. Matthew 11:29.
7. Revelation 21:4.
8. John Ortberg, *Eternity Is Now in Session: A Radical Rediscovery of What Jesus Really Taught about Salvation, Eternity, and Getting to the Good Place* (Carol Stream, IL: Tyndale House Publishers, 2018), 21.
9. Tara Beth Leach, *Radiant Church: Restoring the Credibility of Our Witness* (Downers Grove, IL: InterVarsity Press, 2021), 36.
10. Matthew 20:26-28.
11. John 8:31-32.
12. John 14:27.
13. John 16:33.
14. Matthew 5:44.
15. Luke 12:32.
16. Matthew 6:26.
17. John 15:18-19.
18. Matthew 26:52.
19. John 10:17-18.
20. Colossians 1:13-14.
21. Genesis 1:26.
22. Matthew 4:17 (emphasis mine).
23. Lesley DiFransico, "Repentance," in *Lexham Theological Wordbook*, ed. Douglas Mangum et al., Lexham Bible Reference Series (Bellingham, WA: Lexham Press, 2014).
24. N. T. Wright, *Matthew for Everyone, Part 1: Chapters 1–15*, 20th anniv. ed. (Louisville, KY: Westminster John Knox Press, 2023), 21.
25. Summary of the story of Josephus found in N. T. Wright, *Jesus and the Victory of God*, Christian Origins and the Question of God, vol. 2 (London: SPCK, 1996), 250–52.
26. Matthew W. Bates, *Salvation by Allegiance Alone: Rethinking Faith, Works, and the Gospel of Jesus the King* (Grand Rapids: Baker Academic, 2017), 3.
27. Matthew 4:19.
28. Matthew 4:20.
29. John 17:16.
30. Philippians 3:18-21.

NOTES

31. Dallas Willard, *Hearing God: Developing a Conversational Relationship with God* (Downers Grove, IL: InterVarsity Press, 1999), 220.

CHAPTER 4 | CHASING GRANDER DREAMS

1. Robert X. Cringely, *Accidental Empires: How the Boys of Silicon Valley Make Their Millions, Battle Foreign Competition, and Still Can't Get a Date* (New York: Harper Business, 1996), 185–86.
2. John 15:5.
3. Skye Jethani, *What If Jesus Was Serious? A Visual Guide to the Teachings of Jesus We Love to Ignore* (Chicago: Moody, 2020), 43.
4. John 3:30.
5. Matthew 6:33.
6. Matthew 25:35.
7. Matthew 16:24.
8. Psalm 34:8.
9. 2 Timothy 2:12.
10. Hebrews 12:28.

CHAPTER 5 | LIVING THE SCRIPTURES

1. Twain to Joseph Hopkins Twichell, letter, September 13, 1898, in *The Letters of Mark Twain and Joseph Hopkins Twichell*, ed. Harold K. Bush et al. (Athens: University of Georgia Press, 2017), 220.
2. John 1:1.
3. Matthew 4:1-11.
4. For example: Matthew 11:10; Mark 7:6; Luke 22:37; John 6:45.
5. John 10:35.
6. Leviticus 20:10.
7. This reference is found in the Dead Sea Scrolls and is the earliest mention of the Pharisees in ancient literature.
8. Scot McKnight, "A Conversation about the Pharisees," January 5, 2023, in *Kingdom Roots*, podcast, https://podcasts.apple.com/us/podcast/kingdom-roots-with-scot-mcknight/id1078739516?i=1000592747340.
9. Exodus 20:8.
10. Rodney Reeves, *Matthew*, The Story of God Bible Commentary, ed. Tremper Longman III and Scot McKnight (Grand Rapids: Zondervan, 2017), 112.
11. Mishnah, Shabbat 7:2.
12. John 5:7-12.
13. Mishnah, Shabbat 7:2.
14. Matthew 12:1-2.
15. Scot McKnight, *Sermon on the Mount*, The Story of God Bible Commentary, ed. Tremper Longman III and Scot McKnight (Grand Rapids: Zondervan, 2013), 66.

16. Romans 5:1, HCSB.
17. McKnight, *Sermon on the Mount*, 70.
18. Jonathan T. Pennington, *The Sermon on the Mount and Human Flourishing: A Theological Commentary* (Grand Rapids: Baker Academic, 2017), 177.
19. Reeves, *Matthew*, 113.
20. Skye Jethani, *What If Jesus Was Serious? A Visual Guide to the Teachings of Jesus We Love to Ignore* (Chicago: Moody, 2020), 53.
21. 2 Timothy 3:16-17 (emphasis mine).
22. Romans 14:10-13; James 4:12.

CHAPTER 6 | LOVING RADICALLY
1. *Seinfeld*, season 8, episode 13, "The Comeback," written by Larry David, Jerry Seinfeld, and Gregg Kavet, directed by D. Owen Trainor, aired January 30, 1997, on NBC.
2. Matthew 5:21-48.
3. Dallas Willard, *The Divine Conspiracy: Rediscovering Our Hidden Life in God* (San Francisco: HarperSanFrancisco, 1998), 178.
4. Matthew 5:38.
5. Jonathan T. Pennington, *The Sermon on the Mount and Human Flourishing: A Theological Commentary* (Grand Rapids: Baker Academic, 2017), 195.
6. See Exodus 21:23-35; Leviticus 24:19-20; Deuteronomy 19:21.
7. You can reach the National Domestic Violence Hotline by calling 1 (800) 799-SAFE (7233).
8. Willard, *The Divine Conspiracy*, 175.
9. 1 Corinthians 6:7.
10. Ephesians 4:26 (emphasis mine).
11. Andrew Gross, "Nearly 80 Percent of Drivers Express Significant Anger, Aggression or Road Rage," AAA News Room, July 14, 2016, https://newsroom.aaa.com/2016/07/nearly-80-percent-of-drivers-express-significant-anger-aggression-or-road-rage.
12. Christy Bieber, "Revealing Divorce Statistics in 2024," October 16, 2024, *Forbes*, https://www.forbes.com/advisor/legal/divorce/divorce-statistics.
13. Romans 8:1.
14. Pennington, *Sermon on the Mount*, 191.
15. Pennington, *Sermon on the Mount*, 191.
16. Matthew 19:10.
17. Matthew 5:21-26.
18. Matthew 5:27-30.
19. Matthew 5:31-32.
20. Matthew 5:33-37.
21. Matthew 5:38-42.

22. Matthew 5:43-48.
23. Willard, *The Divine Conspiracy*, 178.
24. See Scot McKnight, *Sermon on the Mount*, The Story of God Bible Commentary, ed. Tremper Longman III and Scot McKnight (Grand Rapids: Zondervan, 2013), 146.

CHAPTER 7 | PERFORMING FOR THE RIGHT AUDIENCE

1. "Oxford Word of the Year 2007: Locavore," *OUP Blog*, November 12, 2007, https://blog.oup.com/2007/11/locavore.
2. Manuel Linares et al., "Selfie-Related Deaths Using Web Epidemiological Intelligence Tool (2008–2021): A Cross-Sectional Study," *Journal of Travel Medicine* 29, no. 5 (July 2022), https://doi.org/10.1093/jtm/taab170.
3. Dallas Willard, *The Divine Conspiracy: Rediscovering Our Hidden Life in God* (San Francisco: HarperSanFrancisco, 1998), 190.
4. Os Guinness, *The Call: Finding and Fulfilling the Central Purpose of Your Life* (Nashville: W Publishing Group, 2003), 74.
5. Willard, *The Divine Conspiracy*, 202.
6. John Calvin, *A Harmony of the Gospels: Matthew, Mark and Luke*, trans. A. W. Morrison, ed. David W. Torrance and Thomas F. Torrance, Calvin's New Testament Commentaries vol. 1 (Grand Rapids: Eerdmans, 1972), 202.
7. R. T. France, *Matthew: An Introduction and Commentary*, Tyndale New Testament Commentaries, vol. 1 (Downers Grove, IL: InterVarsity Press, 1985), 139.
8. N. T. Wright, *The Lord and His Prayer* (Grand Rapids: Eerdmans, 2014), 27.
9. Hebrews 4:16.
10. 1 Peter 5:8.
11. Wright, *The Lord and His Prayer*, 53.
12. C. S. Lewis, *The Weight of Glory and Other Addresses* (New York: HarperCollins, 2001), 26.

CHAPTER 8 | PRIORITIZING THE KINGDOM

1. Ted Scofield, "Everybody Else's Biggest Problem, Pt. 5: You're Gonna Need a Bigger Boat," *Mockingbird*, September 8, 2015, https://mbird.com/everyday/everybody-elses-biggest-problem-pt-5-youre-gonna-need-a-bigger-boat.
2. Quoted in Scofield, "Everybody Else's Biggest Problem."
3. Gautam Nair, "Most Americans Vastly Underestimate How Rich They Are Compared with the Rest of the World. Does It Matter?" *Washington Post*, August 23, 2018, https://www.washingtonpost.com/news/monkey-cage/wp/2018/08/23/most-americans-vastly-underestimate-how-rich-they-are-compared-with-the-rest-of-the-world-does-it-matter.
4. For example, see Matthew 14:13-21.

5. J.D. Roth, "The Cluttered Lives of Middle-Class Americans," GetRichSlowly.org, updated December 5, 2023, https://www.getrichslowly.org/cluttered-lives, quoting Jeanne E. Arnold, "A Cluttered Life: Middle-Class Abundance," University of California Television, video, October 30, 2013, https://www.youtube.com/watch?v=3AhSNsBs2Y0&t=27s.
6. N. T. Wright, *Advent for Everyone: Matthew: A Daily Devotional* (Louisville, KY: Westminster John Knox Press, 2019), 102.
7. Jeannine K. Brown, *Matthew*, Teach the Text Commentary Series, ed. Mark L. Strauss and John H. Walton (Grand Rapids: Baker Books, 2015), 71.
8. Brown, *Matthew*, 71.
9. See, for example, 2 Corinthians 8:2. R. T. France, *Matthew: An Introduction and Commentary*, Tyndale New Testament Commentaries, vol. 1 (Downers Grove, IL: InterVarsity Press, 1985), 143.
10. Jonathan T. Pennington, *The Sermon on the Mount and Human Flourishing: A Theological Commentary* (Grand Rapids: Baker Academic, 2017), 238.
11. As explained in Arthur C. Brooks, "What You're Really Worried about When You're Worried about Money," *The Atlantic*, December 9, 2021, https://www.theatlantic.com/family/archive/2021/12/worry-money-maslow-hierarchy-needs/620950. Referenced survey: Northwestern Mutual, "Planning and Progress Study 2018," accessed October 2, 2024, https://news.northwesternmutual.com/planning-and-progress-2018.
12. United States Census Bureau, "National Poverty in America Awareness Month: January 2024," accessed November 25, 2024, https://www.census.gov/newsroom/stories/poverty-awareness-month.html.
13. Brooks, "Worried about Money."
14. A key clarification: When Jesus talks about worry, he isn't referring to what we have come to know as clinical anxiety. There can be psychological and physiological factors behind worry, and we'd be wise to consult the expertise of mental-health professionals to address those issues.
15. Matthew 6:21.
16. Scot McKnight, *Sermon on the Mount*, The Story of God Bible Commentary, ed. Tremper Longman III and Scot McKnight (Grand Rapids: Zondervan, 2013), 212.
17. Matthew 6:33.
18. Leviticus 27:30; Malachi 3:8-10.
19. Mark 12:41-44.
20. Acts 4:32.

CHAPTER 9 | GROWING IN RELATIONAL MATURITY

1. Amy-Jill Levine, *The Sermon on the Mount: A Beginner's Guide to the Kingdom of Heaven* (Nashville: Abingdon Press, 2020), xi.

2. Dallas Willard, *The Divine Conspiracy: Rediscovering Our Hidden Life in God* (San Francisco: HarperSanFrancisco, 1998), 217.
3. Andy Stanley (@AndyStanley), X post, November 13, 2021, 3:38 p.m., https://twitter.com/AndyStanley/status/1459636689715048458.
4. For more on this ministry, see https://www.communitychristian.org/communityfreedom.
5. From an email to the author.
6. Name has been changed.
7. Galatians 6:1.
8. Willard, *The Divine Conspiracy*, 228–30.
9. Willard, *The Divine Conspiracy*, 229.
10. Henri J. M. Nouwen, *In the Name of Jesus: Reflections on Christian Leadership* (New York: Crossroad, 2024), 77.
11. Todd Rose, *Collective Illusions: Conformity, Complicity, and the Science of Why We Make Bad Decisions* (New York: Hachette Books, 2022), xv–xvi.
12. Scot McKnight, *The Sermon on the Mount*, The Story of God Bible Commentary, ed. Tremper Longman III and Scot McKnight (Grand Rapids: Zondervan, 2013), 255.

CHAPTER 10 | HEARING AND OBEYING JESUS

1. John 14:16-17.
2. John 8:31, NLT (emphasis mine).
3. John 14:23 (emphasis mine).
4. John 6:40, NLT.
5. Ephesians 2:8-9.
6. James 2:17.
7. Danielle Strickland, *The Other Side of Hope: Flipping the Script on Cynicism and Despair and Rediscovering Our Humanity* (Nashville: W Publishing Group, 2022), 124.
8. Scot McKnight, *The Sermon on the Mount*, The Story of God Bible Commentary, ed. Tremper Longman III and Scot McKnight (Grand Rapids: Zondervan, 2013), 265.
9. James 2:19.
10. Genesis 15.
11. See, for example, Exodus 20.
12. Luke 22:20.
13. Dallas Willard, *The Great Omission: Reclaiming Jesus' Essential Teachings on Discipleship* (New York: HarperCollins, 2006), 166.
14. John 10:7.
15. McKnight, *The Sermon on the Mount*, 261.
16. Skye Jethani, *What If Jesus Was Serious? A Visual Guide to the Teachings of Jesus We Love to Ignore* (Chicago: Moody, 2020), 149.

17. See Galatians 5:22-23.
18. Joshua Gardner, "Hidden in Plain Sight: Student Uses Orange Walmart Tie to Help Him Sneak into UVA Huddle Just Before Historic ACC Win," March 20, 2014, *Daily Mail*, https://www.dailymail.co.uk/news/article-2585433/Hidden-plain-sight-Student-uses-orange-Walmart-tie-help-sneak-UVA-huddle-just-historic-ACC-win.html.
19. 1 Samuel 16:7.
20. John 14:20.
21. Quoted in Lee Strobel, *The Case for the Real Jesus: A Journalist Investigates Current Attacks on the Identity of Christ* (Grand Rapids: Zondervan, 2007), 61.
22. Greg Haugh, *Fully Human: Why the Humanity of Jesus Changes Everything* (n.p., 2017), 9.
23. Philippians 2:5-11.
24. 2 Corinthians 5:21; Hebrews 4:15; 1 Peter 2:22; 1 John 3:5.
25. Gerald F. Hawthorne, *The Presence and the Power: The Significance of the Holy Spirit in the Life and Ministry of Jesus* (Eugene, OR: Wipf and Stock, 2003), 35.
26. John 8:36.
27. Matthew 4:19.

EPILOGUE
1. John Stott with Douglas Connelly, *Reading the Sermon on the Mount with John Stott* (Downers Grove, IL: InterVarsity Press, 2016), 108.
2. John 16:33.
3. Matthew 7:12.
4. Matthew 6:20.
5. Matthew 5:44.

DISCUSSION GUIDE
1. Jonathan T. Pennington, *The Sermon on the Mount and Human Flourishing: A Theological Commentary* (Grand Rapids: Baker Academic, 2017), 238.

NavPress
Bold. Loving. Sensible.

Since 1975, NavPress, a business ministry of The Navigators, has been producing books, ministry resources, and *The Message* Bible to help people to know Christ, make Him known, and help others do the same.®

"God doesn't want us to be shy with his gifts,
but bold and loving and sensible."
2 Timothy 1:7, *The Message*

Learn more about NavPress:

Learn more about The Navigators:

Find NavPress on social media:

CP2044